theMotherhood

Jamila Rizvi is an author, presenter and commentator. Her first book, *Not Just Lucky*, was published by Penguin Random House in 2016. Previously Jamila worked as an adviser in the Rudd and Gillard governments and was Editor-in-Chief of the Mamamia Women's Network. Jamila has been named one of Australia's 100 Most Influential Women by the *Financial Review*. She lives in Melbourne with her husband, Jeremy, her son, Rafi, and a lot of clean but regrettably unfolded washing.

the Motherhood

Australian women share what they wish they'd known about life with a newborn

edited by Jamila Rizvi

VIKING
an imprint of
PENGUIN BOOKS

VIKING

UK | USA | Canada | Ireland | Australia
India | New Zealand | South Africa | China

Penguin Books is part of the Penguin Random House group of companies
whose addresses can be found at global.penguinrandomhouse.com.

First published by Penguin Random House Australia Pty Ltd, 2018

1 3 5 7 9 10 8 6 4 2

Cover design by Laura Thomas
Typeset in Adobe Garamond by Midland Typesetters, Australia
Printed and bound in Australia by Griffin Press, an accredited ISO AS/NZS 14001
Environmental Management Systems printer.

 A catalogue record for this
book is available from the
National Library of Australia

ISBN 978 0 14378 357 2

penguin.com.au

To my mother, Helen, for whom children always came first.

And to my original Motherhood, Emily, Ceri and Sarah,
for holding my hand in the dark.

On motherhood:

The biggest gamble in the world.
It is the glorious life force.
It's huge and scary.
It's an act of infinite optimism.
– Gilda Radner

Contents

Introduction

Jamila Rizvi

They warned me that my world would be turned upside down. They lied. My world is not upside down because an upside down world implies that it's still the same world viewed from a new angle. Cars flying through cloudy skies and planes gliding under the sea like submarines, dinner parties hosted on the ceiling and dogs digging holes in the leafy green canopy of trees, that sort of thing. My world is not upside down. It has gone forever.

The world I now inhabit in no way resembles what came before. I am wearing leggings, a nursing bra and my dressing gown. It is 1.42 p.m. and I haven't yet made it to the shower because the baby won't settle unless he is in my arms. My husband is at work and in a few hours time I will start texting him incessantly, berating him for leaving me alone so long. I'm burning mad at him. He has the privilege of being allowed to leave each weekday, whereas I am a caged animal. I live in captivity. I am wild and scared.

I've watched four episodes of Gossip Girl *since midnight and three seasons since the birth but am not properly following the inane plot line. My nipples are sore, my head heavy and the laundry basket is full of tiny piss-stained sleep suits and poo-soaked towels. I have spit instead of perfume on my décolletage and I couldn't say for sure whose it is. Everything hurts, but mostly my broken dreams. I've tripped and fallen into a Truman Show–style loop of awfulness. I have ruined everything.*

A new world, indeed . . .

There were lots of tears in those early weeks after my son was born: many of them mine. Once the visitors began to slow and extended family returned home, my crying rivalled the baby's in both magnitude and frequency. I was swollen and raw from giving birth, still sweating out excess fluid at night. I was confused. I had no clue what I was doing. I was shocked. My mind dealt exclusively in internalised reprimands of how I 'should' be feeling and dark comparisons with how I was. There was a truckload of anger and even more fear. I was frustrated by the happy motherhood lie I'd been sold and convinced that I was the first person ever to go through this. I walked gingerly, afraid of what might happen in my nether regions as the result of a sudden movement. Going out alone was daunting and altogether too hard. I was desperately, desperately, desperately tired.

My tightly controlled life had evaporated. My confident, proud sense of identity replaced with a zombie who couldn't tell day from night. I produced milk like a cow and regularly examined the consistency of someone else's excrement. There was washing to do, always washing to do. My existence was devoted to a tiny human being who was cute but dull company. The reality that the life I'd lived up until then was gone – and wouldn't be coming back – hit me like a punch in the face. I imagined that this was what drowning must feel like. Sitting on our leather couch, I would stare for ages at the burnt-out tea light candles hanging on strings and blowing in the wind outside the living room window. I'd made them after seeing a pretty picture on Pinterest, which the final product didn't really resemble to be honest. I fleetingly considered leaving the house to buy the various crafty bits and pieces to construct them again, but remembered I had a baby now. Crying. My stomach dropped an inch: he was awake again. We were never apart long, he and I, yet it was the loneliest I have ever been.

Two years on, I have superhero-like fantasies about returning in time to console my former self. I would sit her down in the beaten-up armchair, gently curling strands of unwashed hair behind her ears. Taking our baby from her arms, I'd remind her to breathe. When you're at the gym doing a particularly painful exercise or lifting a heavier-than-usual weight, you instinctively hold your breath even though it actually makes things harder. Life with a newborn is similar. You're so tightly wound that you forget to do yourself even the most basic of kindnesses. I know what she's thinking. She's waging a great war inside her head, a battle for acceptance of and acquiescence to the fresh hell that is her new life. Her fear? That it will always be like this. She dares not hope otherwise because the disappointment would be too much. She's bored out of her fucking brain and yet even the quick crossword is too intellectually rigorous to contemplate. It's as if she simultaneously expelled a baby, a placenta and about 30 IQ points from her body during birth.

I want to hold her and fill her with promises of how much easier, how much better it will become. I want to show her the endless stream of iPhone photos and videos of that beautiful baby boy, who has grown into a funny, clever and kind toddler and who will one day become the very best of men. He is, unquestionably, the greatest thing that my husband and I have ever done. But she doesn't know that yet. I want to show her that all this joy lies ahead. I want her to realise it will be okay and that the world will expand once more and she won't always feel claustrophobic and trapped in this tiny apartment with the walls closing in around her. I want to herald a reassuring message from the future that it's true: she will feel like herself again. That she will *know* herself again, and that life will be big and bright and beautiful and loud and luscious once more.

More than half of new mothers report feeling lonely and isolated during the first year of their child's life. Many new fathers experience the same thing. While, thankfully, the physical structure of my home ceased its fuzzy shrinking sensation within about a fortnight, the loneliness of motherhood stayed with me for several long months. As a community we spend an awful lot of time making sure new parents are doing okay in those early weeks. But for some, the first few weeks after birth actually end up being the comparatively easy bit. That's the period when neighbours drop by with homemade lasagne, a partner is usually within shouting distance and relatives flit in and out, leaving washed dishes and cute pastel-hued presents in their wake. Everyone wants to come and see you and see the baby and see the nursery and tell you how well you did and give you a whole lot of unsolicited advice.

But after a week or so they stop coming. And it's just you.

My feelings of isolation were compounded because I didn't have many girlfriends with kids. The birth was a shock and the months that followed even more so. I was utterly unprepared for the seclusion. It's only now that I realise how common my experience was. The loneliness of modern mothers isn't the exception – it's the rule. It didn't used to be like this. It's hard to imagine that a tiger-skin-clad mother would have been left alone in a cave to fend for herself with a newborn for days on end. If her spear-wielding baby-daddy had to go out for a few hours hunting boar or buffalo or dinosaurs or some such, she would have been safe and warm in the company of dozens of other women. Mothers, aunts, sisters, cousins and fellow tribespeople, all taking collective charge of the new family's wellbeing. It takes a village to raise a child and yet so much of modern parenting takes place in silos. Each of us existing within the confines of our individual white-picket-fenced prisons. We limit our support structures to those who are related to us by blood, not wanting to be an imposition on others beyond the time period deemed socially acceptable.

New parents groups provide some relief, but it's not like you can call someone you met ten days prior at 4 a.m. when you're sobbing for the life you used to lead. They didn't even know you then, so how could they possibly understand? Also, they've got their own new baby. Also, you don't want to impose. Also, you're probably just being silly. Also, you should be able to deal with this on your own. Also, it's not like you've got anything in common besides having had sex at roughly the same time nine months prior. And also . . . asking for help is easy to promise but excruciatingly difficult to do. Sharing the load with one another isn't something that we're used to. Help doesn't happen because the community doesn't offer and those who need it don't ask. In times gone by, the upbringing of children was everyone's joy and everyone's responsibility. The trials and tribulations of life with a newborn, a baby, a toddler, and even a teenager, were made easier because they were shared. They were made easier because women did them together.

I didn't ask for help and I dearly wish I had. Thankfully, one friend realised without me having to ask. Clare arrived at the bottom of my apartment stairs, unannounced and ready for action. She had an armful of food and her then nine-year-old twin boys by her side. Instructing her sons to sit and be delighted by my newborn (I've never met nine-year-old boys who were delighted by a newborn but Oscar and Elijah feigned passable interest), Clare went straight to the sink and began washing up. She stayed only about twenty minutes, cleaning the whole time, before telling me I was a champion and walking out the door. One hour later I received a text message that changed everything. Text messages are designed to convey basic information quickly and with no fuss. Back in the days before 4G, you used to pay an extra 20 cents for every additional 140 characters. I remember composing and recomposing messages to my high school boyfriend; declaring my love while sticking to a tight monthly phone budget. Well, if Clare's SMS had been billed under the old system it would have cost her at least $20. This wasn't a quick *Hey cute baby, thanks for the tea, bye.* It was a letter and, oh, what a letter it was.

Clare's kindness filled me up to the brim. Lying in my unmade, milk-spattered bedsheets, I read her wise words and found companionship for the first time since becoming a mum. She understood what I'd been through in a way that my loving, feminist husband never could – try as he might. She understood the interconnectedness of the physical, the emotional and the mental. She had lived the same exhaustion, the loss of identity, the loneliness and the fear of permanency. She described the long, luxurious, uninterrupted eight-hour blocks of sleep I would have again someday like it was soft porn, and I gave myself up to the fantasy. Oh, the sleep fantasy. It pushed every button. She made me promises that others had already, but, for some reason, they only rang true when I heard them from Clare. By sharing her story, she helped me accept the realities of how my would henceforth be written.

Ever since then, I've wanted to devise a way of doing for other women what Clare did for me. I wanted to give the gift of my experience to someone else, to help them feel more normal and less alone. The problem is that the hypocrisy of motherhood makes this almost impossible. What I mean is that motherhood is both a unique and ordinary experience. As mothers, it is something that we share and through which we create bonds and discover commonality. Yet, at the same time, I've had many discussions with friends about childbirth and about raising a newborn where I catch myself thinking, 'Really? Did we do the same thing?' Our tales of a shared time bear so much and yet so little resemblance to one another.

The only solution to this conundrum was to write a book, not about my own story but about many women's stories. So I began speaking with mothers who I love and admire, asking whether they would relate their experiences for the benefit of new mothers to come. I was overwhelmed by how many of them agreed, furious in their determination to make those early months just a little bit easier for someone else. As each letter arrived in my inbox,

I was invited into the quiet, lonely living rooms of women all over Australia. I read with a tightly clenched jaw about the excruciating pain and brutal shock of labour. I laughed aloud at misconceptions and absurd expectations about maternity leave. I shuddered as the memories of completely debilitating, annihilating sleep deprivation returned to me. I sat in silent awe of the unknown challenges and suffering that I was spared. And I was moved by the many and varied descriptions of a love like no other.

Zoë Foster Blake writes with humour and tenderness about not only making a baby but a family. Giving birth in a country far from home, Kumi Taguchi's feeling of isolation was further entrenched by foreign customs. Alys Gagnon is furious at a system that told her 'breast is best' and nothing else would do; she labelled herself a failure before she'd even got started. Kara Keys didn't realise until much later that her bruised and battered experience of new motherhood had been shaped by postnatal depression. Em Rusciano's hilarious account warns against the dangers of mothers' groups, whereas Holly Wainwright insists you should never miss a meeting. Jen Clark and Kirstie Innes-Will are mothers to the same beautiful baby and yet their storytelling is strikingly different. Lanai Scarr writes about the challenges of newborn triplets (yes, triplets) with awe-inspiring optimism. And the divine Clare Bowditch, whose wisdom freed me from the choking seclusion of new motherhood, says birth was the remaking of her and for the better.

Motherhood is famously full of expectations and judgement. We mothers tend to turn on one another in order to justify our own behaviour, when really we're equally scared and unsure of this new rollercoaster ride. We give into our worst selves and criticise one another, when we can be and *are* better than that. The purpose of this book is to share the depth and breadth of the new mother-hood experience, to validate and console new mothers that they are not alone. This book will encourage you to look up from the couch and see a world full of women who are like you, who have been where you have been and who will hold you through the hard parts. My own experience was made bearable only when I found myself a Motherhood: three women whose love and generosity helped me laugh at myself, find joy in my new family and give me reassurance that I was doing okay: Emily, Ceri and Sarah.

Just last month, my family and I experienced one of those perfectly imperfect storms. A dear friend in hospital, my baby sick with tonsillitis, then I caught it from him, all of which caused everyone to fall behind with both home and office work. I was lying in my stinky sickbed, mentally preparing to haul myself up to collect my toddler from childcare, when the phone rang. It was Emily, whose son attends the same centre as my own. Her voice was warm and kind and firm as she informed me she'd be collecting both kids and would be dropping my son home shortly. Later that day, I got a message from Ceri, who lives up the road and wanted to make sure I was okay. Did I need anything from the shops? The chemist? 'Tell us how can we help,' was her loving demand. That night I stayed up late, messaging back and forth furiously as Sarah confessed to her mothering fail-of-the-day. She provided the giggles and the gratitude I needed. They were the simplest of unprompted kindnesses, each a reminder that the white-picket-fenced prison is entirely of our own making. Yes, it takes a village to raise a child and that village is in danger of being rendered the stuff of history unless we rebuild it.

If you're reading this book while sitting at home, with a newborn that you don't quite know what to do with, surrounded by piles of tiny unwashed clothes and confusion, then you have all my love. This part is brutal, it really is, and you shouldn't have to do it solo. Ring me and I'll come around. Seriously. Not with a casserole or a pie, but with a hug and the collective wisdom of this book of magnificently reassuring letters from the women who are now *your* motherhood. We can talk together, we can laugh and we can cry and cry and cry and cry. You are going to get through this difficult period. It is going to end. So, when you feel up to it, take a shower, get dressed, bundle up that baby and venture out into the world. Find the women who are doing this with you, for they will be your salvation. And, in the meantime, the mothers in this book are right here beside you, holding your hand.

Welcome to The Motherhood, my dear.

Rebecca Sparrow

'In the coming weeks and months, as the fog lifts and you feel more like yourself, you will truly see that being someone's mum is like the best song you've ever heard.'

Dear Me,

I want to cry for you.

That's not helping, I know. I should start by saying 'You look great!' or 'Didn't that kitchen reno turn out well! Smart thinking going for the pantry with the slide-out shelves!'

But you look exhausted. And overwhelmed. Plus you have – for the first time in your life – not one but two cold sores on your face from stress and lack of sleep. You look like shit. (Sorry.)

Oh God, I want to cry for you.

Because this first six weeks with Ava – your first baby – is hard. No, hard doesn't seem like a strong enough word. Let's go with brutal.

When they placed her in your arms for the first time, you were flooded with love. Remember? I remember. Your heart was bursting and all you could think was, 'I'm the one who gets to take her home!' as though you'd won some amazing raffle prize.

You were the happiest you have EVER been. You still are, but girl, right now you are also on the verge of collapse.

That beautiful little baby girl never sleeps. EVER. Well, not for longer than twenty minutes anyway. During the night she cries and cries and cries unless you or Brad are walking her around the house. And you, my beautiful girl, are slowly beginning to unravel.

I want to cry for you.

Because you are mentally and emotionally drained. You're trying so hard to follow that EASY routine (Eat Activity Sleep Your time) but that little baby is having none of it. She wants to feed every forty minutes. Her naps are brief and her crying? Her crying, crying, crying is breaking your heart.

I know all of it. I know that you have to wear her in a sling on your chest day AND night. I know how petrified you are of the evenings because you're so tired you're worried you might fall asleep while you're walking around and around and around the lounge room and what if you drop her?

You're madly googling *colic* and *intolerances* and *routines* and *crying babies* for answers. These past few days you've been driving yourself mad wondering if she's allergic to your breastmilk. Your low point was this morning when you went into the chemist with this little baby strapped to your chest (she's ALWAYS strapped to your chest), tears streaming down your face as you stood at the counter wondering what on earth to do. Brace yourself, because in a few days a friend with a newborn includes you in a group email where she raves about how her daughter is already sleeping in loooooong stretches. You read your friend's email and burst into tears.

I want to cry for you.

Because it's really, really hard. You're living in Townsville with no family for hundreds of kilometres, all of your friends are back in Brisbane and you have a husband working night shift as an obstetrician. You are so in love with your beautiful baby girl, but so overwhelmed and so very tired. You feel so alone. It's just you and you have no clue what you're doing and you're terrified you're doing everything wrong.

So what I want to say to you is this: that little girl who never sleeps, well, you won't believe this but she becomes an AMAZING sleeper. Better than that, she grows into the most glorious, enchanting, curious, hilarious young girl.

She is pure joy. Well, most of the time.

When she's four years old you will routinely liken her to Stalin, Idi Amin and, yeah okay, Pol Pot, but that is only because she has a particularly severe haircut at the time and stamps her foot at you a lot. That's also the year she whispers to you that she longs for Peter Pan to come to her window so she can fly with him and Tinkerbell to Neverland.

These days, that little baby who always cries is the eight-year-old girl who always smiles. Your days are spent unpacking playground dramas and reading *Harry Potter* together in bed when her little brothers have gone to sleep.

Her favourite place is still your lap. Her eyes search for you in every crowd. You bake gingerbread together and swim in the pool and go out for milkshakes, and colour in. She is funny and clever and kind and fierce. And messy – her Lego obsession is

OUT. OF. CONTROL. But she is everything you ever wanted or hoped for in a little girl.

And those first six weeks are like some distant land.

So, right now, that's what I want you to know. Right now is *hard* but you can do this. At the ten-week mark that little pork chop starts to sleep (not through the night; that'll take a year . . .) and a few weeks later she'll start sleeping in much, much longer stretches. You will relax and so will she.

You're going to make mistakes. (After a visit to the park with your mothers' group you put her to bed only to discover hours later that she has an enormous brown leaf stuck to the roof of her mouth. Well done, you.) But EVERY new parent makes mistakes.

What I'm saying is – you've got this. HANG IN THERE.

Because in the coming weeks and months, as the fog lifts and you feel more like yourself, you will truly see that being some-one's mum is like the best song you've ever heard. The best party you've ever been to.

It's the beaming smile, the lit-up eyes, the utter joy your eight-month-old baby has when you walk into her room first thing in the morning. It's the lying together in the dark, having a cuddle in bed with your four-year-old whispering about tomorrow and whether Madeline McKenzie is really going to bring a lizard to kindy.

It's the puppet shows and the dance concerts, the netball practice and the stories. It's the crayon pictures – where you've been depicted with pink hair and your head is strangely eighteen sizes too big for your body – that will crowd out your fridge door. It's the cuddles and hugs and kisses. The 'you look so beautiful, Mama' comments when you know – actually – you're so tired you look like your passport photo.

It's the rituals and the traditions that *you* get to create or continue for your own little tribe. Her habit of saying 'Hold my handle' or asking if fairies are inside the traffic lights turning them from red to green.

It's the fact that this little person trusts you implicitly, loves you unconditionally and BELIEVES in you more than you would ever believe in yourself. It's the continual moments and chances to show Who You Really Are.

It's all of that. And then some.

Now sucks. I get that.

Is motherhood easy? Nope. Nopety-nope-nope.

But it *is* amazing. Just wait. The song, my dear girl, is about to begin.

Bec

Zoë Foster Blake

'You were simply shattered from the most enormous and athletic endeavour your body had ever undertaken and you wanted some goddamn shut-eye. Surely the reward for pushing a human out of the vagina is a nap?'

Dearest Zo,

First of all, I don't care what anyone says: I think those tracksuit pants look lovely. I like how you've teamed them with a knit (and a *bra*! Fancy!), so that people will take you seriously.

Now. How *are* you?

I gather from the tears and the chocolate that you're maybe still getting your head around this whole newborn thing. Zozo. This is *perfectly normal*. But I think that *maaaaybe* that is part of the problem: you didn't know what would be normal. In fact, you had no concept whatsoever of what this first three months would be like! Who friggen does? No one.

Here's why:

A. It's impossible to adequately articulate the astronomical upheaval that a newborn brings with him or her. Friends with kids just kind of look at you with their eyebrows raised and say, 'Life will never be the same again, that's for sure!' before laughing nervously. This is partly because they know it doesn't help to say that it is FUCKIN' FULL ON but also because they have completely forgotten what it's like. Just as nature intended;

B. You were too tunnel visioned on labour/birth to pay any of this shit any mind; and

C. You figured it would all come naturally, like in documentaries about tribal mothers who just intrinsically know what to do once they give birth.

Don't worry.

Your charming ignorance is classic first-time mum stuff: you spent the bulk of your pregnancy reading up on calm birth (yes), water birth (maybe) and perineum massaging (no) in preparation for fifteen hours or so of labour and birth. And you spent *zero* time researching what to do once you get home with a small, helpless human who wails for milk every three minutes, and a vagina with PTSD.

Remember how cute that midwife thought you were when you said how you were gonna sleep all day once they'd taken freshly born Sonny off to be cleaned up. She was wiping away your vomit, because you had asked for toast even though they said you would probably vomit it right back up, but you REALLY needed some toast.

Oh, how she giggled.

You weren't to know that your new son would demand to be fed every two hours (yes, even through the NIGHT) and that you wouldn't get a block of more than four hours sleep for many weeks. You were simply shattered from the most enormous and athletic endeavour your body had ever undertaken and you wanted some goddamn shut-eye.

Surely the reward for pushing a human out of the vagina is a nap?

But sleep would have to wait.

As you soon discovered, you had more important stuff to do! Like learning how to make your enormous nipple fit into your child's teeny mouth and dispense milk, and also you needed to cry a lot. Joyful crying, frustrated crying, overtired crying – all the flavours of crying.

Your birth experience was a happy and positive one, and you are right to think of it fondly. But the direct aftermath was a bit fucked, wasn't it? You were foggy from the drugs, freshly stitched up below, and copped a bitch of a nurse who yelled at you about how cold the hospital room was, and snapped that Sonny should be in a *wool*, not cotton, blanket, and if you didn't figure out how to breastfeed him soon, his blood sugar levels would drop danger-ously low. (Since you had gestational diabetes, your baby's blood sugar levels *were* crucial those first few days, but, weirdly, being bullied and panicked into learning how to breastfeed wasn't a *super* effective teaching technique.)

Once *she* fucked off, things got way better. A kind, funny, patient midwife (like 99 per cent of midwives) showed you a latch technique that worked and that didn't make you cry or feel hopeless.

Gestational diabetes wasn't all bad, though. Since you hadn't had any sugar for months (before then the sweet, golden crutch helping you through a busy and stressful pregnancy), you were nutritionally in good nick. And now you had permission to undo all of that in one sucrose-dense banquet.

Cue the post-birth reward you'd been talking to your husband about for months: cupcakes, croissants with jam and butter, Haigh's freckles and, to replace some of the energy lost in child-birth, a giant, hot meatball brioche sub. Not a slice of sashimi, soft cheese or champagne in sight.

That first week with Sonny was bliss. He seemed to think he was still in utero. Life was good. You had your darling husband by your side, lots of lovely visitors, no pressure to be doing anything other than looking after your child, and the power-ful hormonal love bubble protected you from sleep deprivation madness.

Do you remember how once you were home – and the swollen, puffy, foggy aftermath of your labour drugs had finally worn off, and you were able to stop putting ice packs into your big, saggy black undies – how happy you were? You'd made a baby, but you'd also made a *family*.

It was unseasonably warm for May, the house was dappled in sunshine and bursting with blooms . . . even the cat seemed more affectionate than usual. You sat contentedly on the couch, breastfeeding your boy, wolfing down tea and toast, curious as to who he was, and how life would be now, and just how you had managed to pack his hospital bag so hopelessly wrong. (Next time: Bonds Wondersuits only. No fancy shit.)

But all too quickly, shit got real. Days and nights rolled into one, showers became a luxury, and as you struggled to deal with a baby who cried always and slept never, you sent your husband out to buy every book about newborns and sleep routines available, and proceeded to drive yourself, and him, mad by attempting

to force a ten-day-old baby into a feeding and sleeping routine.
IDIOCY.

As you soon realised, before they are twelve weeks old babies
don't give a fuck about routines. They do whatever the fuck they
want and you are helpless to do anything about it.

Witching 'hour' is the perfect example. When you read that
part in a psycho sleep book about the period from five to nine
each night, when babies cry nonstop and suddenly develop the
appetite of a fifteen-year-old boy, and the author said to only feed
the baby *twice* in that period so as to 'train' them, and you and
Sonny both ended up wailing, because *of course* that shit didn't fly,
because, as you now know, witching hour is just the baby loading
up on food so he or she can sleep longer overnight, or, in other
words, there is a REASON for it, but you were trying to fight that
very real reason, and getting more and more upset as he lay there
bawling in his bassinet, hungry and distraught.

Oh, but you were so desperate for some normalcy to return to
the house! In shock and grieving for nights when you could have
some dinner with your husband and watch *Survivor*. Instead you
now had a wailing, confusing mini human in the house that you
were forbidden to feed or settle, according to some obnoxious
author tyrant.

You googled ENDLESSLY. Was it reflux? Was it your milk
making him unwell? Should you be cutting out dairy and onions
and garlic? What was the answer? *Why did none of those fucking
forum mums have the answer?!*

Best thing you did was bin those ludicrous books, and get
offline, and ask a real, live midwife for actual advice on your actual
baby. It was gas, like most babies that age. The digestive system is
deeply unsophisticated before six weeks, and fast and furious milk

flow combined with your sweet pig of a baby's appetite meant he was full of big gulps of air and unable to sufficiently expel it. Hence: upset and uncomfortable. (Willby's, Infacol and Infant's Friend was of *great* help: *remember to tell all other new mums about it.*)

Anyway. I guess the lesson was: there are no rules in the first six, or even twelve, weeks. You do whatever works. All that eat-sleep-play shit comes in later. There will be months of sleep training and routine stuff* to come. For now, flop out a boob, grab a snack and get comfortable.

Now. Regarding your daily almond croissant habit. It *might* be time to go easy on the treats. I know you're rebelling against the taste deprivation that GD brought with it, and you're VERY VERY HUNGRY ALL THE TIME, but don't let cheese toasties and muffins and cakes and milkshakes do all the heavy lifting. It's horseshit, all that stuff about breastfeeding burning millions of calories. In most cases, lingering post-baby weight gain will be nothing to do with the baby and everything to do with the cookies. (Yes. Even the lactation ones. *They're still cookies.*)

Another reason to eat well is that your immune system needs a hand. Case in point: the mastitis you had when Sonny was two weeks old. And didn't it swoop in like lightning!?! The swollen, hot boob, the fever, the instant and intense melancholy . . . you were just shy of being hospitalised, and all because you thought you could skip a feed and not express. *No.*

That nasty mastitis will keep coming back, unfortunately.

---

* A baby on a routine is definitely what you need, by the way. It's not for everyone, but it's really, really for you. You're a person who needs predictability in your day, and while babies are pretty much the antithesis of that, getting a routine in place is your best shot of finding some structure in your life and your ability to do your work.

It's a Foster woman thing. Our tits can't take the heat, apparently. Don't be afraid to talk to your doctor about antibiotics, but try not to use them unless shit gets really bad/the fever kicks off. Next time you feel your boob getting warm or hard: feed that baby, feed, feed, feed, and massage the boob as you do to help unblock the duct causing you trouble. Also, use a hot compress before feeds, then a cold compress afterwards. Take Nurofen and powdered Vitamin C and good probiotics and *rest*. Fuck the washing. Fuck emails. Just rest, you sweet goose.

People say that at six weeks it gets easier, and it does. It also gets easier at twelve weeks, six months, and then again at forty years.

Hang in there!

You're doing great. Make no mistake: this is VERY hard, and a huge adjustment. You're a woman who is used to being in control of your day, your time, your sleep, your workload, your home, your body and your boobs, and now a small, cute, loud child has come in and wiped his sweet yellow shit all over that. It will take time to adjust. Years! And he will keep changing. Just as you think you're mumming good, he will wake up a completely different beast.

I know right now you are feeling the failures hard, but just ask any Instagram quote or tattoo: *this too will pass*. You and your boy are in good health, every day you learn something new and helpful (mostly from texting other mums), your new business is just fine without you helicoptering over it 24/7, you have discovered a new concealer that kindly grants you the illusion of a pulse, and you and your husband are still (mostly) civil to each other despite the utter destruction of your sleep, house and life as you know it.

There are lots of golden moments. Lots.

This is parenting. You are DOIN' IT! Be proud of yourself. Go easy on yourself. Love and look after yourself. Don't be a hero. Don't be a martyr. Don't be a jerk. Ask for help. Take the wins when they come. Cuddle and sniff your son nonstop. Don't assume everyone else is having an easy time of it, or is better at it than you, or is having WAY more fun than you. And don't be unkind to your husband because you're tired. He is parenting too, and he's very good at it, actually.

I love you.

You've got this.

Also, your hair could do with a wash.

Zoë xxx

Clementine Ford

'I've always been fond of small, wrinkled humans, but I realise now that it was in a temporary and superficial sort of way. I liked babies in the way you like a novelty tattoo or a bikini wax.'

Hello there, me from a different life,

It is a great luxury that the conceit of letters written to past selves allows the current selves writing those letters to skip around and address the various iterations of our constant selves at different points in time. When I sat down to begin this letter there were two different versions of me that came to mind . . .

The first was the version of Me who sat waiting for lift-off on the precipice of the unknown (very uncomfortably, I might add – those last few weeks of pregnancy are no joke). Perched there, in the in-between of being still myself and being someone's mother, I waited, folding tiny baby clothes. Oh, and watching a lot of *Hoarders*.

Oh dear, naïve, waiting pregnant past-self! Go to the movies! Sit in a park and look at the clouds! Drink a cup of hot tea and enjoy the fact that it stays hot!

Because then there's the second version of me, the Other Me.

She's the one who's just given birth to my first child, the one who's collapsed in a house that looks like a hurricane ripped through it while running away from a tornado, in despair over the fact that all the tiny clothes are covered in shit and spew, and who is just generally *fucking terrified.*

Shhh, terrified past-self New Mother Me. Take a deep breath, and heed my promise: *it's all going to be okay.*

I can scarcely believe I'm writing those words down because it seems like mere moments ago that I was in exactly the position New Mother Me was in. That is to say, curled up in a ball, crying and shovelling mini Mars Bars into my mouth. I'm kidding, of course. My newborn would never have allowed enough space to accumulate between his and my body to afford me the room to adopt the foetal position. But the part about the crying and the Mars Bars is true.

Let's back up a little bit, to the time before that cold winter's afternoon when my vagina tore apart and I pooped out a baby. Did I say out? I meant on. I pooped *on* a baby – because the twin tunnels tend to converge as one when a boulder smashes through them. Of course, he has pooped on me – and my clothes – numerous times since then and at least twice on jeans that I probably didn't wash in-between. Still, I take some small solace in the fact that I did it first.

As I was saying, dear past self, the time I spent preparing for a baby did nothing to actually prepare me for a baby, aside from providing a visual memory of the last time my house would ever be truly clean. It's not that I didn't have some vague idea that emotional destruction and babies go hand in hand – it's just that I didn't really understand that my baby would *actually* be a baby.

I've always been fond of small, wrinkled humans, but I realise now that it was in a temporary and superficial sort of way. I liked babies in the way you like a novelty tattoo or a bikini wax. While pregnant, I fantasised about my life as a mother, but these daydreams never included visions of the excruciatingly difficult newborn period. Instead, I preferred to skip straight ahead to the time when a cherub with chubby thighs could sit up and giggle and thus present a viable financial stream on YouTube.

And yet, there I suddenly was, with a very newborn-ish newborn, shell-shocked and physically wrecked and completely, utterly perplexed as to how a team of medical professionals allowed me, serial killer of plants, to take him home. As I sat there on the freshly made bed that would slowly morph into a funk-filled nest over the next few weeks, I gazed down at the blotchy, squishy creature curled up next to me.

I've made a terrible mistake, I thought.

As quickly as I felt it, I squashed the feeling down. In the past, my anxiety had been like a wild horse whose body I was strapped to. It could flare up at any moment and gallop off, me furiously trying to hold on for dear life, never certain when the terrifying, nauseating ride would end. I had spent much of my pregnancy strapped to that bucking beast, but something about the monumental act of childbirth had fortified me and in that moment, looking down at my baby, I felt the power shift. I had broken the horse and I was the rider now.

Still, being in control of my anxiety didn't necessarily lessen the general fear of new parenthood, nor did it make it any easier to reckon with the imagined idea of a baby versus the reality. Here are some things that I learned in those early months:

1. Breastfeeding

Discard everything you think you know about breastfeeding. The images of serene women sitting in tastefully decorated nurseries, bathed in the dappled sunlight that treacles in through the branches of a sturdy oak tree outside. Breastfeeding, if you choose to do it, is fucking torture. The period of time for which it is torturous may vary (some get away with a couple of weeks, others endure months of it), but you can rest assured that torture is part of the learning curve.

Your baby may have a tongue-tie that will need to be snipped in order to help their latch. Very luckily, ours was identified and dealt with on Day Two, which made the whole exercise a little less confounding but had no bearing on the unfortunate fact that nipples in their restful, non-food provision state, are not meant to be sucked on for hours each day. Oh yeah, your baby is going to feed for at least eight hours of every day. Breastfeeding a newborn is a full-time job and do not ever let anyone tell you different.

The other hot tip is to squeeze a little milk out and dab it into the area, then hang out topless for a bit. Breastmilk is a wonderful antiseptic, and you can file that away for the time you get conjunctivitis on a tropical island at Christmas time and alternate your miserable hours squeezing antibiotic cream into your eyes and just squirting milk straight into the corners while everyone else drinks beer in the pool downstairs.

Cracked nipples are no fun, nor is the moment you look down at your suckling baby and see blood smeared all over their face from the crevices that have been carved into your most sensitive areas (the blood won't hurt them, though). But if your latch is okay and your supply is all right, I think in most cases it *does* get better. It took about ten days for the pain to disappear for me and my supply seemed to be fairly well established by the end of week five. Hang in there, pal.

2. Cluster feeding

You are about to find out that you didn't just bring a baby home from the hospital – you brought their zombie alter ego. Zombie Baby appears somewhere between the hours of 3 p.m. and 7 p.m. and stays until either just before midnight or just before dawn. They gnash and snarl at your breasts for what feels like days, draining you both physically and emotionally. Fun times!

Cluster feeding is horrible but it's necessary to help you establish your supply. Your baby is stimulating the production of more and more milk so they can ensure their survival. But, hey, it's still a really tough and anxiety-inducing time. It's okay to know that it's necessary and also to hate the process itself.

There may be times when cluster feeding makes you feel like you hate your baby a little bit. You may feel a tired and impatient urge to rip them from your body and throw them across the room. Enduring cluster feeding also shows you what you're capable of. Each night when the zombie appeared, I felt like I couldn't handle a single more second of it. And just before I felt ready to give up, the hunger broke and he slept. I survived and it did pass.

3. Babywearing

Consider getting a baby carrier or a wrap. I was very determined while pregnant that my baby would mostly travel in a pram because I believed then that we parents could control what babies like, want and need. Then I had a baby who hated being in his pram, because sometimes he hated being put down. Amazingly, my baby wasn't content to hang out alone and untethered, because he was a tiny baby who had spent nine months only knowing my smell and my sounds. I could choose to fight his will or I could surrender to it.

Babywearing made everything so much easier. He slept like a champion when curled up next to my warm body. Whenever he was tired or stressed out, being snuggled next to me immediately seemed to calm him down and make him feel safe. I spent a lot of time walking the streets of my neighbourhood and patting his little bottom. And I feel like it really helped me to establish the bond with him that I had missed out on through the horrendous months of pregnancy anxiety. It turned us into a team. Plus, it's heaps easier to get on and off a tram.

4. Breathe. You've got this

You can do this. You really can! Babies have been surviving for thousands of years and in much harsher conditions than your Australian house! You won't break them or irreparably harm them if you don't attend to their cry immediately. If you need five minutes for sanity, take it – put them in a safe place and just leave the room for a breather. They will be okay. Speaking of being okay, babies are much more pliable than we think. My policy was to take the level of gentleness I felt needed to be used and remove 25 per cent of it. Wrestle them into their clothes, because you won't get them in by treating them like a wet noodle.

5. Surrender

I spent a lot of my first six weeks as a mother seeking reassurance from friends with older babies. *Is this normal?! When do they stop doing this?! When will they sleep?!* It's hard not to feel freaked out by the massive responsibility of newborn rearing, particularly when your experience of babies is limited to making faces at six-month-old laugh factories in cafes.

As hard as it would be, I was advised to surrender to it all. These early days are overwhelming, intense and scary at times, but they are also so, so, so transient. Babies really do grow and change every-day, and you find that the saying is true – the days are long but the weeks are short. Unexplained crying peaks in intensity at six weeks and it's all downhill from there (with new and different challenges!)

6. Enjoy it

Cuddle them skin-to-skin, listen to their funny coos and squeaks, take a grillion photographs of them in exactly the same position. Look forward to their first smiles, because nothing melts you faster than realising they have an emotional spectrum beyond tears and gas.

7. Embrace the opportunity to learn about yourself

I remember seriously yelling at my partner at about Day Seven (a particularly bad zombie feeding night) that I wanted a Grown Up to come and help us. But, as he reminded me, YOU'RE the Grown Up now. You can be scared of that (and it's okay to be sometimes) but you can also find courage in it. And, hey, the really liberating thing is that figuring that out makes you realise your parents didn't know shit about shit either.

8. Trust your instincts

You can read as many books as you like. Make all the lists you want, buy the things that people say you need, listen to the experts.

It won't make a lick of difference, because your baby can't read and hence doesn't know what they're 'supposed' to be doing. If you want to feed to sleep, because that's what your baby responds well to, do it. If you want to co-sleep, go for it (we did). If you don't want to do either of those things, that's your prerogative: *you are the boss.*

If you discover, as I did, that your tiny newborn baby will only go to sleep on your chest and not in the bassinet you've set up as a sidecar on your bed, then just let it happen. They won't be sleeping there forever. There were many nights I woke up with a start, convinced it had been dangerous to let us both snooze in that position, only to find him curled in the same spot and my arms wrapped in a vice-like grip around him.

Do what works for you. And remember, there is no real 'normal' when it comes to your baby because they are completely new beings that have no expectations of anything. Babies are balls of pure instinct. All they need from you is for you to love them and feed them and change them and keep them warm and make them feel safe. You are their normal.

9. This too shall pass

You'll hear this a lot over the next few weeks. You won't believe it at first because you probably also feel like you've fallen into a black hole of time where everything stays the same for the rest of eternity. There will be pre-dawn pockets when all you can hear is the sound of the street sweeper outside and the little sucking noises of your baby and you'll think to yourself, *This is all there is. I was born in this room, I live in this room and I will die in this room.* Then you'll make some more online purchases because that's what you do at 4 a.m. when a baby's feeding.

But I assure you: this too *shall* pass. And one day you'll find yourself looking at a baby who's sitting up, then crawling, then walking, then learning to speak and you'll think, *Where did all the time go?* It's here. Right now. You're in it. This is the time.

Dearest Brand-new Mother Me of the past – and all the brand new mother yous reading this – Close your eyes. Trust your instincts. Be brave. Let yourself fall. Love is there to catch you, and it is bigger and stronger and more powerful than anything you've ever known.

Clem

Alys Gagnon

'You will come back from the darkness and you will be surprised by how quickly. You will very soon be able to look into the face of your own child and feel explosive, warm, jolly love for that baby: love that is no longer tainted by anger.'

Dear Alys,

Guess what? A future version of you has just spent half an hour staring into the faces of your two sleeping children, trying to decide if you truly are done, trying to decide whether you want a third.

I know that right now that seems unbelievable. You aren't quite sure you can handle the single tiny bundle of a child that lies in your arms. You're half convinced that the hospital made a grave mistake sending you home with *A Baby*, an actual real life bona fide child, one with ten fingers, ten toes and a red, squished-up, wailing face. What were they thinking?

The idea of being responsible for not one child but per-haps three children is beyond your befuddled, sleep-deprived comprehension. And yet, the adorable, cheeky face of your three-year-old Claire and the serious, studious expression of your six-year-old William will prompt you to question your lifelong commitment to just two children. What's one more, after all? They're so freakin' cute.

But, right now it feels like you have been airdropped. Alone. Into Southern Tanzania. Then the authorities, some faceless, nameless officials you have no way of contacting, have shut the airports, closed the train stations and blockaded the roads. You cannot leave. You're sure that this is a very nice place most of the time, but you can't help panicking because this life is so thoroughly different to that which you are used to. The slow realisation that there is simply no way out of this is moving you perilously close to the precipice of depression.

You've always known you're susceptible to it, depression. It's the family history, and throughout your life so far there have been plenty of times you've felt it creeping up on you. Usually you remember your depression is really quite mild and you take some simple steps to try and stay healthy.

But right now, things are different. Right now, you're stuck.

Your simple steps revolve around giving yourself control and creating order among the chaos inside your head. You write a to-do list, clean the house, eat more vegetables, get some exercise, some sleep and some sunshine. But at the moment you can't do any of these things. These things have to be sacrificed at the altar of on-demand feeding and constant newborn care – not that there's anything in your breasts to feed your child when he constantly demands it.

You're not quite sure why the natural, normal way of feeding a baby isn't working for you. After all, you did all the right things.

You read all the pregnancy books and all the baby care books. You went to all your prenatal classes, including the optional breast-feeding class. You practised a breastfeeding hold with the dolly, in a circle of women who were all holding dollies to their breasts while staring blankly in the room, trying to pretend this was a perfectly normal way to spend a Tuesday afternoon. But your caesarean section, your teensy inverted nipples, your gigantic bosoms – so big they dwarf the baby in front of you – and your child's total lack of patience to learn how to latch have all combined to made breastfeeding nigh on impossible.

Poor boy, it wasn't his fault. He was hungry.

The first person to gently suggest William get formula was the paediatrician at the hospital, who could see he was turning yellow with jaundice and that his sodium levels were creeping unacceptably high – both symptoms of dehydration. It was an awful moment. You had to ask the midwife to take the baby from you so you wouldn't drop him. You turned in on yourself, curled up to sob whole body sobs and howl ugly howls. You will still shed a tear when you recall the moment years later.

You'll read the accounts of women who breastfed, who say they felt so engorged with milk that it hurt, and you are totally mystified about why your own breasts remain completely pain-free. Someone will describe the let down to you and they may as well be describing life on Mars for all you've ever felt trying to squeeze droplets of milk from your own body.

You will watch a friend feed her newborn and see her nipples – they're three times the size of yours and stick out like marshmallows on top of cupcakes – and wonder why God gave you breasts so big they require bras designed by civil engineers but nipples so small they look like they belong on a child.

You'll try expressing, but as exhaustion descends, and you spend two hours at a time feeding a baby and then attaching the milk machine to your empty breasts like a cow in a dairy and hoping against all hope that you'll get more than 20 millilitres of breastmilk, you'll feel like you're on a fool's errand.

Soon William will be fed exclusively with formula, and though without it he will fail to thrive, you have bought into the social idea that good mothers breastfeed and bad mothers don't. That's hardly surprising. After all, in a system that is designed to promote breastfeeding as the best choice for babies, the silent implication is that formula is second best. Therefore, you think to yourself, mothers who don't breastfeed are depriving their children.

You're panicking, you're depressed and you're more tired than you have ever been before. You're doing mental gymnastics trying to come to grips with giving your baby formula at the same time as fighting the idea that you're a terrible mother who doesn't deserve her baby. You're in a wave of hormonal emotion that you've never experienced and you're certain there is nothing you can do to stop it.

And so you play to type, you descend to cliché and you become the wounded animal. You're cross with anyone trying to tell you what to do: nurses, midwives, lactation consultants, maternal and child health nurses, friends, family. You oscillate between nervous wreck and angry maniac.

'This is fucked', you think as you declare that you will give up any attempt at breastfeeding for good, ten days in, and go cold turkey. You do so against all medical advice.

'Fuck them', you think as you pack away the breast pump for the last time. 'Fuck them', you mutter while opening the shopping and methodically stacking away the tins of formula and cheap dummies. 'Fuck them', you wail inside yourself, as you boil water and meticulously sterilise the teats. 'JUST FUCK THEM', you silently shout at your hungry baby who finally gets what he needs.

And because your baby's tummy is full, he sleeps. Finally, he sleeps.

And so you get some sleep too.

The sleep should help, but it doesn't. Rather than coming up for air, you descend further into your fury, convinced still that no one has ever been through what you've been through, and that no one will ever understand how you feel. You move past constructive emotion and become irrationally enraged. You're so angry with everyone around you that you become angry with perfect strangers.

Pity the poor woman you will run into at the shops. She's asking for donations to support the valuable work of the Australian Breastfeeding Association and, rather than politely declining and moving on, you will lash out. It's as if her very existence serves only as a reminder of your angst-filled decision to switch to formula.

Pity the poor midwife who visits you at home, the one who you will glare at with steely eyes as she hands over the required leaflets that explain how to re-lactate. It's just her job, Alys. She doesn't know your situation. It's not like she hasn't seen half-a-dozen new mothers earlier in the day, and it's not like she won't see another half-a-dozen after you. She's overworked and underpaid.

Pity the people on Twitter . . . At the time when William was born, Twitter was a different place. These days it's a chamber of shouty, but back then there was a lot more listening and learning and conversation happening. So at four o'clock in the morning, with a baby in your arms, bottle in one hand and phone in the other, you could regularly be found checking in with the #3amfeedclub crew.

You must have been following people who were very serious about promoting breastfeeding because, somehow, during one of your early morning scroll and feeding fests, you found yourself in the middle of an involved conversation. It was led by a group of lactation consultants and revolved around the marketing of infant formula and the promotion of breastfeeding.

They were discussing new ways of supporting mothers to breastfeed, ideas they had heard at a recent conference. Some of them were describing individual cases they had been involved in, how they had helped mums who desperately wanted to breastfeed to keep going on their feeding journey and, in particular, how they had helped these mums deal with the pressure placed on them to give up, and switch to formula.

Scrolling down through the feed, down, down, down, merely mirrored your own descent. Down, down, down you went. With every new tweet, you fell further and further into a haze of anger, unable to see that these women were simply discussing their own experiences, and that they were not judging you.

Finally – and probably very predictably – you lost control. You inserted yourself into the middle of a considered conversation of professional women. You were convinced that they were attacking you *personally* with their mundane chitchat about the World Health Organization Infant Formula Marketing Guidelines. You opened Twitter and typed accusatorily at them: *All I am seeing is 'la la la, give your baby formula and you may as well give it heroin.'*

Alys, I say this with an awful lot of love: but not everything is about you.

You are not the first person to have had a baby, and you're not the first person to have struggled to feed her child. Women have struggled with breastfeeding since the dawn of time. Where once there were wet nurses, communities of women who fed each other's babies without a second thought, there is now formula. Your breastfeeding struggles do not make you special or unusual. And that's a good thing.

During this particular part of your life, you don't want or need to be special. The best thing for you to be in these early weeks of motherhood and caring for a newborn is perfectly ordinary, perfectly average. Take comfort in the fact that you are far from alone. Stop for a moment and see the truth of your situation.

Close to half the world's population have been exactly where you are at some point. You're one in a billion. You're one in many billion, in fact, and many of those billions struggle to feed their newborns. Because once you find comfort for yourself, you will be able to see the comfort that everyone around you is trying to offer you and the women just like you, going through exactly the same thing, at exactly the same time.

There is hope for you yet, Alys. You will come back from the darkness and you will be surprised by how quickly. You will very soon be able to look into the face of your own child and feel explosive, warm, jolly love for that baby: love that is no longer tainted by anger. You will find joy in the chaos of your life, your out-of-control house and your newly complicated schedule and your messed-up bank accounts. These things will take on new meaning, because with them comes the gift of watching a small person grow.

And, yes, you will find yourself a slave to an overwhelming urge to have more babies. You will have one more, and you'll fight an internal battle over the possibility of a third for years after that. You'll be tempted by the love of holding a baby in your arms, the chance to rock her to sleep in the middle of the night, to feel the warm drowsy sweetness of a midnight formula feed.

Take a deep breath my darling and do what must be done: forgive yourself.

Alys x

Jessica Rudd

'Here's what I have to tell you about motherhood: if you are lotto-level lucky, it will never end. You will be mothering until the day you die.'

Dear Me,

Dear me, indeed. This is a tough one.

It has taken precisely twelve months to write these twelve hundred words. I've written entire novels in half that time, but this isn't a tale packaged up into neat chapters lit by the sparkle of an overactive imagination. This is something fuller, messier and ongoing.

I've found myself asking why on earth I agreed to expose myself, to expose us, like this at all. Yet here I am, waiting while the car is being detailed, coffee in hand, kids with my husband, and I am watching a woman who is just like us.

Her car is behind mine in the queue. One of her newly scuffed boots is unzipped, revealing an under-elasticised sports sock.

She tugs a dryer-lint-covered black nursing top down over the top of her maternity jeans. Her muslin-wrapped bundle squawks like a macaw and refuses the breast as she stares longingly at her now-cold flat white. She sits two tables over and looks desperate to slip back into her car – her travelling office – but she has to wait. Here.

A hungover man slurps at his Coke, plays a game on his phone, then goes to the loo.

Our girl glances up. We know what she's thinking, of course.

There was a time when she could be hungover, last night's shoes strewn down the hallway. Phone dead. Keys lost. Head sore, but content in the knowledge that she has all weekend to recover on the couch with *Game of Thrones*. There was a time when her bladder and bowel took turns at dictating toilet trips. Now someone else's organs call the shots. And, oh, to send a multisyllabic text!

'Let that lady go first,' I say quietly to the bemused bloke with the chamois.

He does not compute what I am suggesting.

'The lady with the baby,' I push.

He points to an overhead screen listing number plates in order of priority.

'You're next. Or do you wanna cancel?'

I look at the line of cars behind mine.

'Can't you just put her in front of me? Swap the order?'

'Sorry, mate. You can't override the system.'

Ain't that the truth.

I think that's what I found most confronting about those early weeks of motherhood. It doesn't seem to matter how evolved you are, how much your partner or family want to help or how urgently you need to get back to work – the first twelve weeks are pretty much you and bub. That's it. It's a natural system that cannot be overridden.

Millennia of human wisdom attempted to remind us of this in every book, at every baby shower, in every unsolicited gem of advice, but it's hard to heed a warning that doesn't align with basic principles of justice and fairness. Wasn't it supposed to be liberté, égalité, maternité? Or something kind of like that . . . ? My brain doesn't work any more. #sleepdeprivation

The point is, new motherhood seems to come as something of a shock when it should be anything but. There you are, sweetheart. Babe to boob. Everything you ever hoped for. A healthy child, a home of your own, pastels aplenty. You've even managed to get her name down at a school already, for crying out loud. And yet what the actual fucking fuck? This is so. Bloody. Hard.

You have two questions for me, questions you can't ask anyone else:

When will it end? And, will I ever be me again?

I'll answer these sequentially for ease of reference.

When will it end?

Darling heart, it's not going to end but it will get better. Now I want you to take a deep breath and contain those sobs, because this whole mess is a bit like anti-ageing. Nobody likes grey pubes, incontinence or wrinkles. They're decidedly un-fun. But what's the alternative? The alternative, unless you're Benjamin Bloody Button, is pushing up daisies and we both know you're claustrophobic. I am pro-ageing because I am anti-death.

Here's what I have to tell you about motherhood: if you are lotto-level lucky, it will never end. You will be mothering until the day you die. You will have babies who become healthy children, healthy children who become obnoxious but healthy adolescents, obnoxious healthy adolescents who become freeloading, healthy housemates and freeloading, healthy housemates who become the healthy parents of your healthy grandchildren.

At this point in your life, especially in those first six weeks, this is not something you'd want to read on the brochure, but I can tell you, babe, that there will be times you'll want to hit pause and soak it all in. There will be those skin-to-skin endorphin surges, when your lungs flush with warm air, your heart is awash with happy beats. There will be times you glance down at tiny fingertips and marvel at their plush pink perfection. You'll see her seeing you, cognisant that you are her epicentre and she is yours. She will smile and you will beam. She will giggle and your eyes will moisten with joy.

And that's all within the next few weeks, I promise.

Then it gets even better. She will pat your back reassuringly when you stub your toe. She will applaud your warbling nursery rhymes in the car. She'll inhale instead of blowing out her first birthday candle and it'll be the cutest thing ever. She will stand on tippy-toes and lick the wooden spoon as you make cupcakes for kindy.

And then one day she will lower her heels and you'll see her forehead above the other side of the island bench and you'll think, *What's she standing on?* But she isn't standing on anything. Suddenly, her arms drape down your back when you carry her asleep from the car to bed. She says things you didn't tell her and teaches you things you ought to know about the pyramids, Maori language and animation. Then she's in a uniform, her back-pack down to her calves, hat swallowing her head, and you'll be thinking, *Whoa, Nelly – slow down.*

Where you are now, you're not thinking slow down. You're desperate to get to the magical twelve weeks when the books say it all gets easier. These are your forty days and forty nights. You're in the desert, my love, feeling a bit forsaken and shell-shocked. My words might seem like a mirage, but they are fact. You will get there.

Will I ever be me again?

Here's the executive summary, because you probably need to pump or pee or eat: no, you'll be better than you. You will be me. (Modesty has never been my forte.)

The whole motherhood thing is utterly transformational. The verb 'father' has come to mean to ejaculate and fertilise. Done. The verb 'mother', on the other hand, means to gestate, give birth, nurse and raise the next generation. The brilliant part of this, and the bit nobody ever tells you, is that you will receive no greater professional development training in your career than motherhood.

Since I began mothering, my productivity has quadrupled. Gone are the days of prolonged Facebook toilet sessions and Friday night office drinks to be regretted on Saturday morning. The new and improved me is stronger, wiser and more efficient.

Next week I am going on a business trip. By the time we are wheels down in Sydney I will have dressed and packed for three people – myself included. I will have completed two drop-offs and filled two lunch boxes. I will have done my meeting prep the night before and organised for the dog to be walked, grass cut and groceries delivered. Sure, I'll look a bit like an Edwardian chimney sweep thanks to in-car eyeliner application and general sleeplessness, but there will be few others at the luggage carousel texting the nanny while doing a conference call and booking an Uber.

There's a deft art at work each day when you are a mother. And to think so many of us doubt ourselves when we return to work! You are far more capable now than you've ever been. You've acquired new skills and honed old ones. You are now boss.

In other news, you'll be pleased to know our confidence is off the scale. Motherhood has cured any self-consciousness we once had. Gone are the body image issues, public singing shyness and conservative dance moves. Nowadays, we could Nutbush on the beach with considerable bikini fuzz, humming show tunes and give hardly any fucks. This is a revelation.

Best of all – and you know this already – the love is and always will be stratospheric. That heady, all-consuming devotion to another being won't wane, but you will get better at balancing it with your own needs, thereby becoming an even better you.

Back at the car wash, our friend with the squawking bundle is shifting her gaze between agitated infant, queue placement and the ladies' with equal disappointment.

I approach her.

'How old is he?'

'Six weeks,' she says, rising to bounce him to sleep.

'You're doing beautifully,' I say.

As you know, this is something our mum says to every single new mum she meets. Now I get it. You probably do too. *That* is all you need to hear.

'Look, this is a bit out of line,' I offer, 'and I won't be offended if you say no, but if you wanted me to hold him while you go to do a wee or enjoy coffee I'd be very happy to. I have two of my own.'

'Oh thanks,' she says, desperate to check my references and immunisation record. 'No, it's okay. That's very kind of you though.'

'No worries,' I say, returning to my seat to keep writing.

Two minutes pass.

'Actually,' she says, pacing towards us and thrusting the now unwrapped baby into our arms.

I laugh. 'Go for it,' I say. 'What's his name?'

'Hugo,' she says, rushing for the ladies'.

'Hello, Hugo.'

I hold Hugo upright. He hates it.

I hold Hugo tummy down. Hates that too.

I put him on my knees and wrap him firmly, arms in, then hold his ear to my chest. Muscle memory. The old girl's still got it.

Hugo hates that less.

Within minutes, the scrunched scowl becomes a cherubic pout. He startles. A hand attempts to escape the swaddle. I go to tuck it back in but all five of Hugo's fingers wrap around one of mine. His breathing steadies. His grip loosens. He lets out an unedifying fart, and the tips of his straight dark lashes reach the peaks of his cheekbones just in time for his mother to return from the loo.

'Show off,' she says, reaching for her coffee.

'He just let out a ripper fart – no poo – and nodded off.'

'Thank God.' She slumps into her seat.

'Want me to put him in the pram?'

'No, I'll take him. He likes to be held.'

'Drink your coffee,' I say.

'Your car is ready,' she says.

'It's fine. I'll hold him. Drink your coffee.'

The heady scent of new human confuses my ovaries, blurring the harder memories you're making today and polishing the rare precious moments until everything else fades into insignificance.

I am you, my darling. And one day soon you will be me. You will become the mother holding another woman's baby and wondering whether, despite it all, you might even go again.

Love,
Me

Kumi Taguchi

'Please love yourself enough to be unapologetic about what you need. Do everything you can to kick the back-of-the-line narrative out the door.'

Dear You,

I am finding this letter hard to write because I don't know how to address you. Because you are me. If you were a friend, I'd use your name. I'd probably start the letter with 'Dearest . . .' or 'My dear . . .' and be crystal clear about how I am here for you and how you need to put yourself first.

But showing the same care for you, for me, for us, feels much harder. Why is it that we can show the utmost empathy and concern for others, yet struggle to justify doing the same for ourselves? I'm hoping to change that, which is why I am writing to you.

When I look back at the first few months after our beautiful girl was born, I wish I had done it differently. Had I known a few more things I would have been a more confident mother and better able to adjust to my new identity. Armed with some insights, I would have been more upfront and pragmatic about asking for support.

You know those moments when life shifts on its axis without warning? A phone call to inform us that someone has died, a letter to say we have lost our job. There is a before and there is an after. Having a baby is different. There are nine months of warning. I remember being acutely aware that life was never going to be the same after the day I went to hospital to have our baby.

I was three days overdue, and in Hong Kong that is a big deal. Not so in many other countries, I have since learned. But the doctors there wanted me to be induced. It's a strange thing, waking up in the morning knowing you are going to have your baby that day. The scheduling is so neat and tidy for something that isn't at all neat or tidy.

I took a deep breath and as I closed the door on our Hong Kong apartment I knew that when I next opened it, my life would have forever shifted.

I left as Kumi, I would return as a mother.

To get her here was not easy. The birth was pretty horrific and I ended up with bruises all over my arms and legs, caused by doctors holding me down because I was writhing in so much pain. Apparently the way I gave birth was like women did in the 1950s: drugs to induce the baby, lying on my back, legs in stirrups.

I remember screaming and saying I understood why women died in childbirth. There is nothing more levelling than that process, knowing you share an experience with women through the millennia. It was frightening.

I wish I had been more forthright about what I wanted. I remember meekly asking a doctor whether I could choose to have the baby in a certain way, meaning a certain position. I was thinking of my friends back home, having active births, home births and using baths and all else. The doctor in Hong Kong responded vaguely, giving me nothing. I sensed I didn't have as many options. So I went along with the status quo and didn't make a fuss.

Overshadowing that whole time was a deep worry about money and how much it was going to cost to have our baby. Everything in Hong Kong was different to home. You either went to a public hospital where nobody spoke English at all or took the super-expensive private option. Being a serial put-yourself-at-the-back-of-the-pack person, I found something in between: a nice, clean hospital with caring staff.

But, as I'd find out later, they did things very much by the book.

Protocol took priority over the mother's wishes.

I wish I'd valued myself enough to push for an option that suited me: the one I really wanted but convinced myself I didn't need. I guess I am telling you this because it was the first tangible signal that I was thinking about others and not myself in that critical time when our girl was first entering the world. That decision was the first in a series, which became a pattern of putting my own needs last.

Our beautiful girl was born and she was healthy and so was I. It is amazing how the trauma of birth dissipates so quickly once you set eyes on your tiny human being. Our little girl had a length and a weight and she was given a name, which was texted to family and friends. That time in hospital was so surreal, it was like living on another planet. I couldn't quite believe this person was 'mine'.

She was perfect.

I don't remember the food or any other minutiae from hospital: only that the place was sterile and cold. I had the first night off from feeding and caught up on sleep. I remember waking up and remembering that I was now a mother and it was all so bizarre.

When I think back to that time, I am struck by the fact there were not many visitors. I could count on one hand the number of people who came to see us over the three days I was there. I didn't have close friends in Hong Kong. I had been living there less than a year before our daughter was born. It was a lonely time. The corridors were dark at night, the sounds unfamiliar. I was in a ward with mothers who didn't speak English.

I walked home from the hospital and when I opened that familiar front door, life was different.

I remembered that it was my birthday; my thirtieth birthday.

It's a milestone usually celebrated with fanfare, so when I opened the door and saw there were no balloons or flowers or piles of presents, it really hurt. The occasion didn't feel at all special. I didn't feel special. I pushed down the disappointment.

I wish I had celebrated our birthday. I wish I had made it a big deal. I wish I had felt special and cherished and loved. I wish I had told those around me that I wanted to mark that moment in time and that I needed their help to do that. I wish there had been some closer friends around me during those difficult early weeks and on that important milestone birthday.

Kumi, I want you to know that I remember that loneliness.

So from me, now, happy birthday.

In the end, the highlight of the birthday was my milk coming in. My breasts were so incredibly huge that I thought they were going to burst. I was in pain and could not get our daughter to feed. In desperation, I called a lactation specialist to come to our apartment. I felt vulnerable and hopeless and exposed. She was kind and got it all going; she was seriously my saviour. I have told countless women since then to have someone on hand to help. It just didn't cross my mind that I might run into problems.

Next began the relentless feeding and sleeping regime. Every two to three hours a little cry would tell me to drag myself from a strange slumber. I went from being someone whose time was my own to someone whose time was someone else's. You don't have a choice and, while nothing will stop you from keeping a child alive, it is the most jarring adjustment I have ever had to make.

There were times in the darkest of night when I would look at that little face, happily feeding and being nourished and nurtured, and I could put aside that tiredness. Thinking back, I am amazed at what I did: having a baby in a foreign country, no friends or family around, buying groceries from new supermarkets and finding doctors and a place to live. But back then, I felt a bit useless.

Once the flurry of cards and presents from home die off, it becomes more quiet, doesn't it? The days were long. I spent a whole morning trying to take a passport photo of a little baby who was only a few weeks old and couldn't hold her head up. The guidelines for the photo were very specific: eyes open, head straight, looking ahead. Not an easy task! I felt guilty for 'only' achieving that one photo over the course of a whole day. I felt like I wasn't useful, that I had not done enough.

Let me tell you, you do and did do enough.

I hope you can feel comfortable with just being. Looking out that window, over the skyline of a wonderful city, and telling yourself, I am here. This time will pass and then there will be another phase and a different phase and other challenges to overcome. But for now, in these early days of this new person's life, take the time to be with yourself and with her. Guilt-free.

Buy yourself a beautiful teapot or, better yet, ask someone to buy one for you. In it, brew a wonderful fruity tea and savour the smell and the time you take for yourself to drink it. If that little voice cries out for you, wait a few more moments and take another sip, and another, and another, and another. As much as you can, grab back small moments of time for you.

I know this is so hard. I know you like to act for others. I know you say you don't need help when really you do, but please try. Try to ask. Please love yourself enough to be unapologetic about what you need. Do everything you can to kick the back-of-the-line narrative out the door. Surround yourself with people who encourage you, who care for you, who drop food onto your doorstep, who ask what they can do to help.

And if there is no army, say you need help in building one. Or fly friends and family over. Or move back home for a while. Do something. Please. You will need it and you deserve it. I need you to put yourself first, for once, if only during this time. That way, you will enjoy it all so much more, or at least have support around you that will prevent you becoming lonely and isolated.

Kumi, one morning soon, you will dress your daughter in a white suit with stripy green tights underneath. You'll prop her up on the big cushions on your bed and will chat to her while you're folding some washing. You'll smile at her as you have done for days upon days, without receiving much in return. And suddenly, like life pivoting on an axis, she'll smile back.

There's a before and there's an after.

Love,
Me

Anna Rose

*'That thought is a scar you'll have for a long, long time.
It's a thought that will make you realise how thin the line
between coping and absolutely not coping really is.'*

Dear Past Anna,

The first six weeks with your baby are going to be spent counting down the days until those six weeks are over. It's kind of like that period towards the end of Year 12, when the days dragged on slowly, listlessly and painfully. Time stretched out thinly, like old chewing gum, towards the end of high school. Summer and freedom were in your sights – so tantalisingly close. But first you had to get through the hard part.

Back then, you and your friends had chalked a tally board onto the brown brick wall next to where your group sat at lunch. Each day, you took turns with the chalk, literally crossing off one more day. It felt like it would go on forever. Like you'd never be free.

And then, suddenly, the hard part – the exams and the stress and the long hours studying – was over. You emerged on the other side, blinking in the sunlight, like butterflies from chrysalis, into a totally new phase of life.

During the first six weeks with Robbie, you can't *wait* for the hard part to be over. Unlike at the end of high school, you're not counting the days until summer flings and surfing. You're counting the days until life becomes liveable again. Because it's so much harder than the last few weeks of Year 12. For starters, you're getting a lot less sleep.

You will wake up every forty-five minutes – or sixty minutes if you're lucky – mostly to breastfeed Robbie. He needs to be fed constantly. And then he'll vomit it back up. And then need to be fed again.

The breastfeeding app on your phone that you use to track feeding times will record an average of three thousand minutes per week in these early weeks. That's fifty hours a week. More than a full-time job. And that doesn't count any of the time pumping, or sterilising the pumping equipment, or holding him when he falls asleep on your chest after feeding. Moving him off your chest is out of the question – he'll just wake up and start screaming if you try.

You'll remember, bitterly, how the maternal and child health nurse had cheerfully told everyone in your prenatal class that one of the great benefits of breastfeeding was that it was completely free! *FREE!?! Only if you value women's time at exactly zero. Including time you could be spending sleeping.*

It's hard to warn you how devastating the sleep deprivation is going to be to your state of mind, your sense of self and your ability to cope. You'll have a constant underlying feeling of desperation. Desperate for sleep. Desperate for Robbie to sleep. Desperate for some time to yourself, but too exhausted to do anything with it when you get it. Desperate for your eyes to stop burning and aching from being so, so tired.

Desperate for food too – you're going to be ravenous. You'll remember this story you once read about how a team of polar explorers replaced sleep with food when they needed to cross the Arctic in a short period of time before the ice melted. Getting through each day in these first six weeks is going to feel like a feat equivalent to crossing the Arctic. Better make sure your fridge is stocked.

If you're not waking up to feed Robbie, you're waking up because you're worried that he hasn't woken up. Anxiety will be pulsing through your veins. You'll have this terrible thought that maybe he's stopped breathing and you should go in to check he's still alive. You need to. Right now. But maybe, just maybe, maybe you shouldn't . . .

Because if he's dead, then at least you can sleep again.

The first time you thought this, it stunned you. Terrified you. Writing now, two years later, you still can't believe it was an actual thought your mind created. Of course, you didn't really mean it. You always went in, every time you woke up, to check he was okay.

But that thought is one of the scars that remains seared into your mind from these first six weeks. A scar you'll have for a long, long time. It's a thought that will make you realise how thin the line between coping and absolutely not coping really is. It's such a far cry from what you ever in a million years expected to feel during this time.

You don't have many friends who are parents, but those few who are promised these first six weeks would be a precious time.

One friend said it was like a beautiful cocoon, ensconced in your baby and your partner, blissfully removed from, and unaware of, the real world.

Well, you'd give *anything* to go back to the real world. Back to your old life where you could take a shower. When you could make a cup of tea without it getting stone cold while you hold the baby on your chest for hours and hours because he will sleep nowhere that isn't on you. Where you could decide what to do with your own time, not be the slave of a tiny, screaming, irrational being.

The real world was where your mind didn't run around in circles thinking of all the things that could go wrong – no, that *will* go wrong, that are *already* going wrong. Feeling guilty all the time. Feeling frustrated all the time. Feeling incompetent all the time.

In the real world, you used to feel competent. You used to *be* competent. In the real world, you set up advocacy organisations that changed the game on the politics of climate change. You recruited thousands of members. You crafted cutting edge environmental campaigns. You managed teams. You ran meetings. You organised rallies. You lobbied politicians. You made speeches. You wrote books. You inspired people. You knew what you were doing and loved learning it when you didn't, and you want that back almost as desperately as you want to sleep right now. You loved your work. It didn't feel like work. It felt like being part of a movement.

But none of that matters now, because you have a real-life member of the next generation vomiting all over you, and screaming. It's as if all of your accomplishments mean nothing. All of the skills you developed over the past two decades of professional life are useless. Worse than useless, actually. Not only are they completely non-transferable to this alien situation you find yourself in, they feel like they're getting in the way of being a good mother. The personality traits that made you good at your work – being an impatient, outcome-driven, extroverted Type-A personality – are the opposite to what is required to be a parent.

You have to deprogram your brain. Learn to structure your time around your baby's unpredictable feeding and nap times, rather than a schedule. Learn to get comfortable not 'achieving' anything by the end of the day. Try to ignore your craving for stimuli in the form of a new email or an article or the satisfaction of crossing something off a to-do list. Become familiar with feeling ineffective and out of your depth. You blunder at simple tasks like changing a nappy. Leaving the house, putting on the baby carrier, and even folding and unfolding the pram feel beyond your mediocre parenting abilities. You're not used to feeling like this. You used to tackle hard challenges. Now you just give up. And even with your very loving, supportive and involved husband doing an enormous amount, and your amazing mum around the corner helping so much too – compared to your old life it's so lonely.

You used to be part of something bigger. Now your world has shrunk to the size of around twenty square metres: the bedroom where you spend the torturous non-sleeping nights with Robbie, the kitchen where you scramble to assemble food, the laundry (more on that particular place of hell later) and the bathroom, where you cry in the two minutes you occasionally get for a shower every few days. Sometimes you venture out into the backyard. Those are good days.

Nothing you've done previously prepared you for these six weeks.

You should have spent your time reading books about breast-feeding. And baby sleep and settling patterns. Maybe you could have spent a fraction of the time you spent in meetings about campaign strategy actually hanging out with parents, learning from their struggles and supporting them.

You just wish you'd known it would be this merciless.

You would have prepared. You've always been a planner.

You could have bought a deep freezer and spent the last few months making food, because then you'd be able to eat. There's no time to cook now. You're crazy for thinking there would be. You could have organised a cleaner to come every few days, because then you wouldn't be having panic attacks about how messy the house is getting and the fact that no matter how many loads of laundry you do, the pile just keeps growing. Robbie has reflux and he vomits on everything. You had no idea how much washing you'd be doing.

In your fatigued state, you find yourself glaring wildly at the laundry pile, building it into a nemesis. In Greek mythology, there's a story about Sisyphus, the king of Ephyra. He was punished for being deceitful by being forced to roll an immense boulder up a hill, only to watch it come back to him, repeating this action for eternity.

Your laundry pile is *exactly* like this.

You could have found a postnatal doula who might have helped you during this crazy time. You'll never need more help than you do during these first six weeks of Robbie's life. You could have figured out a plan to mix breastfeeding with formula feeding if breastfeeding every hour at night was affecting your sleep and sanity to the point that you feel you're going to die from exhaustion. You could have learnt about postnatal anxiety, so you could go to the doctor before it gets so bad that you can't function any more.

Anna, the motivational sayings aren't enough to get you through this time. You've written them on post-it notes and stuck them around the house: in the bathroom and on the fridge. Your favourite Chinese proverb: *Those who say it can't be done should get out of the way of those already doing it.* The one you came across from Winston Churchill years ago: *Never, never, never give up.* And your favourite all-rounder, able to make you smile in most situations: *If Britney could survive 2008, I can make it through this day.*

None of them mean anything when they come up against a brain sodden with sleep deprivation and riddled with anxiety.

The only thing that's going to work for your family, Anna, is sleep training. But that's months away and he's too little now. There'll come a time when both you and Robbie are ready to do it. Please don't fear it. Look forward to it. It's going to save you, and make Robbie happier as well.

Slowly, slowly, slowly you'll become yourself again. He will stop crying all the time. You will stop crying all the time. You will be able to leave him with a nanny or at childcare and do things for yourself again. Like go see a movie, speak at a conference, get back into your work, travel for meetings. You'll stop thinking of him as the cluster bomb that ruined your life. Instead, he'll become the absolute *best* thing about your life.

It seems like a long way in the future from where you are now, but it's not. You'll go from feeling like you can't manage, to one day realising you can and you are. It might happen around six weeks. Or it might happen a little later. Or even a lot later. But there will come a day when you get a little more sleep and then it won't seem so bad. It will keep getting better from there. Now, from the future, after two rounds of sleep training, I can reassure you that he sleeps through the night *and* has a three-hour nap during the day.

It. Is. Amazing.

Soon enough you'll be *loving* the time you spend with Robbie. He'll start engaging with you more, and before you know it he'll be talking enough to have a conversation with you. He's going to grow into such a great little kid. So much fun. So many laughs. The most amazing bond between the three of you in your little family. You and your husband agree every month after about four months: this must be peak cuteness. But he just keeps getting cuter! And when he says 'I love you mummy'? Wow. You wouldn't trade being a mum for anything. You have so much to look forward to. You really do.

The scars from those first six weeks have faded enough now, in the future, that you're even considering trying for a second child.

This is a powerful testament that you can (and will) rebuild your life even after it's been shattered into a million pieces by those first six weeks. Remember that now: it must be worth it for people to go through this hell and still choose to do it again.

For the time being, get as much help as you can. Spend these long days with the other mums you meet at parents' group. That way you won't feel so hopelessly alone in this city where you can count your number of old friends on two fingers.

Try to bring your expectations in line with reality. There'll be some good moments in these early weeks, but mostly it's going to be rough. Ignore all the old ladies who tell you to enjoy this beautiful time. It's not beautiful for you and that's fine. You and your baby will both survive the first six weeks and that's enough. Around the world, many women and babies aren't so lucky.

This is going to be hellish for you, but you're going to make it through.

It's going to be okay and in the end it's worth it.

All my love,
Future Anna

Nicky Champ

'You will find yourself staring at this tiny creature tucked up like a miniature pink bean in her bassinet, willing her to put on weight. People won't coo at her like they do other babies.'

Oh hey there preggo,

You know how your instincts told you that you were going to go into labour early? You know how your obstetrician said 'First babies rarely come early'? You know how you said 'Sure, whatever' to your husband, Matt, flying to Perth a month before your due date?

Spoiler alert: you're going to have your baby four weeks early.

In the middle of the night.

Alone.

And you'll drive yourself to the hospital while having contractions.

So, now might be a good time to start reading *Baby Love*, packing a hospital bag and moving those birthing classes forward.

Your waters will break at 11 p.m. You'll be so tired you'll just want to go back to sleep but, at Matt's insistence, you'll call the hospital. You'll oblige when they say to come in for a check-up. You'll arrive at the hospital at 1.30 a.m. (it took awhile to pack a bag of useless things), but you aren't just going in for a check-up. You won't be sent home on antibiotics to come back at a more sensible time, in, say, four weeks. Less than four hours later, you will have a baby.

Now prepare yourself for the next mic drop: there is no time for drugs.

Not that you had a solid birth plan in place, but you were confident that if it came to it drugs would be on the menu. So not only do you give birth alone, there will be no time for an epidural. So those CalmBirth classes you were looking into? BOOK THEM NOW. You won't be calm. You will be so delirious (or maybe lightheaded from sucking the life out of the gas) that you will consent to four trainee nurses being in the birthing suite documenting the carnage.

Documenting . . . with cameras. Yes, that's something you'll agree to and, no, it is not a decision that someone of sane mind makes. When one nurse pats you on the shoulder afterwards and says, 'Thank you so much for letting me be part of your birthing experience' you'll turn to your obstetrician and mouth the words, 'Who the fuck is that?' Those first three minutes after birth will come to sum up your entire parenting journey to date: bewildering as hell.

It's a girl!

But you can't announce it yet, because her father is still on a plane somewhere over Western Australia and that's 3000 k's away. He's asked you not to reveal the gender before he gets to the hospital. A task that proves a little tricky given that you're technically due at the office in an hour's time. Worried you'll spill too much information, you decide to send a vague text to your boss that went something along the lines of: 'Erm, just had the baby, won't be coming into the office today. KBye!'

In the melee of midwives, trainees, and medical staff, nameless baby girl (later, Amelia) is whisked off to the Special Care Unit. Underweight, and not interested in feeding, the next time you see her she will be hooked up to a myriad of tubes and monitors.

You'll wrongly assume you'll be given a moment to collect yourself and comprehend the situation, but you're told it's time to hop off the bed and take a shower. *Wait, we're doing what now? I'm not even confident all my body parts are on the inside.* Any hesitation you had ends immediately after you step inside the much-too-small industrial-plastic shower cubicle. You're about to have the best shower of your life. Stuff those double shower-heads in five-star hotels, the post-labour shower is right up there on your hospital stay's highlight reel. Even if the trainee nurse does accidentally join you while trying to adjust the water temperature.

On day two, you're going to get mistaken for a nurse and you are not going to take it well. Aside from never wearing navy blue to a hospital again, this only contributes to you feeling like a total imposter.

Other mothers are wheeling their babies around the ward exhaustedly, trying to stay awake and attempting to nail the whole breastfeeding thing. While you're shoving Arnott's twin pack biscuits into your face and pretending it's okay to watch daytime television, while your baby is being tube-fed formula to stay alive.

If your room wasn't filled with pink flowers and teddy bears, you'd think it was a rehab stay. At this point, you'll even take that baby next door who cries constantly day and night.

No one imagines their first moments of motherhood will involve a brisk and determined midwife awkwardly milking their boobs to draw two tiny drops of colostrum into a syringe. Or sitting on a beige vinyl chair in the Special Care Unit at 4 a.m., suction-cupped to a double breast pump. Even six years on, the mechanical 'mmmrrrrttt . . . mmmrrrttt' whirring of a breast pump can still make you shudder.

Not sensing your fragile emotional state The Husband (he finally turns up) talks you into doing a baby settling class. You hide up the back of the room for fear you'll be called on to demonstrate something. Some new mums attend with their partners, some are alone, but everyone has an actual, you know, *baby* with them. Everyone, except you.

You get a few odd stares and become convinced everyone is looking at you thinking, 'Hey Lady, YOU FORGOT YOUR BABY!' You last all of three minutes in that room. Don't stress, the Special Care nurses will teach you everything you need to know. It's the one perk of having a premature baby.

Even though research wasn't your forte leading up to the birth, you have some loose notions of what motherhood is going to be like. You know, the sort of naïve ideas that you laugh at years later. They include a lot of rules, like: no dummies, no formula, only organic wooden toys.

Once the feeding tubes come out, the midwives give Amelia a dummy to help her develop the sucking reflex. A skill she didn't develop in utero due to her swift and early exit. And in with the giant cherry dummy, out goes any preconceived notions of this parenting gig you ever had. In her first few days of life, Amelia has had both formula and a dummy – two things you swore you'd never use. It's like the Birth Gods are sending you an early signal.

There is nothing more surreal than checking out of a maternity ward and leaving your newborn baby behind. *Am I missing something? Wait, didn't I just have a baby?* Credit to the reception staff, who don't eye you suspiciously or question that you don't seem to have a baby in tow. You make it to the tranquillity garden outside before you burst into tears.

The tears are a combination of leaving without Amelia and that she threw up her last feed. It's completely your fault. The frustrated midwife will say you didn't keep her upright long enough. At this stage, feeds still take over an hour (don't worry, it does get shorter), and you will now have to come back in an hour and do it all over again. You'll think that you're not cut out for this; you'll think you can't do this, but you can and you will.

The next week is a blur of four-hourly feeds and waking up in the middle of the night, driving to the hospital to express and driving home again to sleep. All around you, life is carrying on as normal, while you adjust to your new norm of expressing, sterilising, feeding, expressing, sterilising, feeding ad nauseam.

While checking out of the hospital without your baby is one of the most surreal, mind-numbingly awful experiences of your life, it's actually a good thing. Hear me out. Over the next two weeks, those amazing Special Care nurses will set Amelia into a four-hourly routine. You won't realise it until Sam (the baby who comes along nearly four years later) wakes up every two hours for the first YEAR of his life, what an absolute blessing her start to life was.

Next comes the twice-weekly weigh-ins.

For the next three months, you'll trudge up to the local Early Childhood Health Centre to be assessed every Monday and Thursday. By this life stage you've interviewed celebrities and spoken in front of large audiences, but nothing makes you more nervous than the community nurses. *What if they can see through the façade I'm putting on? What if they decide I can't do this?*

Your fears are soon realised. Amelia is not gaining weight. In fact, she's losing it. You haven't got this. You're failing. Why didn't anyone let on that breastfeeding was so bloody hard to master?

After evaluating your feeding technique – at this point you've had more women touch your boobs than boyfriends – the nurses prescribe even more top-up feeds. Which means even more pumping. There's no question that the round yellow machine sitting atop a pile of unread magazines hasn't been another piece of useless baby accoutrement, it's been a constant bovine-like companion.

While you're desperate to go back to work, you have never had a more important job. You take to it with gusto. Your breast-milk stash takes up the entire freezer. You're running out of room for the peas. Matt's so impressed with your efforts, he shows it off to visitors like a game show host. Only weeks into this gig, you've already made the classic faux pas every new parent makes: not realising that no one is as interested in your baby as you. Especially friends who are yet to procreate. Dammit, we were going to be cool parents.

You will find yourself staring at this tiny creature tucked up like a miniature pink bean in her bassinet, willing her to put on weight. People won't coo at her like they do other babies. One relative describes her as 'alien-looking'. (Thanks Dad, I've never forgotten that.) You will see healthy chubby babies everywhere and feel strange pangs of jealously.

Relax. Eventually the weight stacks on and by age two she'll catch up to the rest of the pack. Well, she'll try to catch up, but her roly-poly Michelin Man legs will slow her down. Yes, it's hard to believe now but she will soon have those much-pined-for delicious rolls of fat on her legs and arms. And then some.

Because you had to restrict visitors at the hospital, the entire world is now keen to visit you at home. A task you don't take too well to. Inside the newborn baby vacuum, things are rosy. She feeds, she sleeps (it's early days – ha!) and you view anyone who wants to step inside the bubble with suspicion and a million questions.

Are you sick? Are your vaccinations up to date? What about the whooping cough booster? Oh, you're bringing the kids too? Great. Have they had all their shots? Oh, they have a bit of a cold? Nope, absolutely not.

It's winter, so anytime you venture outside in those early weeks it is a feat requiring seventeen blankets, several changes of clothes, bottles, dummies, nipple shields, nappies and a special kind of origami skill to fold the pram into the back of the car.

You almost don't go to your first mothers' group meeting. It's been raining, it's cold, and bad things could happen outside the bubble. Plus, *you know*, pram origami. At the insistence of Matt you go, but decide if you can't fold out the pram, then it's straight back home with #noregrets.

It's going to take a few weeks before you think of these strange meetings as fun, but near the end you'll start to look forward to them. You've heard the stories about mothers' groups, but you will luck out big-time. You'll know you've found your tribe when, on your first night out together, one mum will turn to the group and say, 'Okay, tell me I'm not the only one who shat on the labour table?'

There'll be no pretending this gig isn't a hard and thankless task. That those first milestones and smiles often don't make up for the total upheaval of what used to resemble your life. Thankfully, no one will be interested in the one-upwomanship game of who can make the most edible organic food purees or bragging about how little Johnny is the first to walk/talk/evacuate his bowels in a socially acceptable place.

Those early playdates spent endlessly discussing what 'new thing baby has done this week' will soon feature wine and thankfully less talk about bowel movements. Although, it really did seem interesting at the time, *didn't it?* These six women will become your sounding board, your moral compass and your tequila-swilling besties. Together, you'll celebrate making it through the first year intact, second and third pregnancies, and you'll commiserate about miscarriages, navigate themed birthday parties and have each other's backs when sanity is in short supply.

But before you go feeling like you've got this . . . just a heads-up. Matt is about to tell you that he's going back to his fly-in fly-out role, leaving you on your own with a newborn baby for up to three weeks at a time. You'll take it on the chin, outwardly confident, but internally you're shitting yourself. How did you not discuss how this might be a problem beforehand? It's not a blip, but an oversight that affects the next four years.

You can and do handle it. Everyone survives, but ask for more help. When your friends want to pop over, let them. Do not give a stuff if your apartment looks like crap. Full disclosure: your house is not going to look any better six years later when it's full of toys. Do not try to be some kind of Stepford Wife/Martha Stewart version of yourself.

Motherhood is a grim task without a village, and you have been lucky enough to be blessed with an awesome one – let them in.

Despite the emotional whiplash, those first utterly exhausting and bewildering six weeks will be some of the most magical. I don't need to tell you to treasure every moment, it'll only make you feel guilty all those times you begrudge this tiny wilful human invading your home. Those times you lose your shit because you have no idea why she's crying and you can't make it stop.

I'll only say: take a breath, put her down safely and leave the room for a moment to collect yourself.

When you can, get out of the house. Go for a walk. Grab a drive-through McDonald's coffee. Listen to a podcast. Forget the baby music classes and do something you both enjoy instead. It's going to be four long years until you get the glorious privilege of doing this all over again.

Nicky x

Sarah Harris

'You'd roll your eyes at impossibly gorgeous Hollywood celebrities like Gwyneth Paltrow, who smugly confessed they'd battled cravings of "crunchy apples and spring water". You could have eaten Gwyneth herself, with the right seasoning and a side of potatoes.'

Dear Sarah,

You look a bit ridiculous.

There you are, sprawled on the bed, one week after pushing out a baby. You're sweating and swearing and struggling to squeeze your broken and bleeding body into a pair of medical-grade compression tights. Your doctor hasn't recommended them. Some svelte mummy blogger did.

The tights are supposed to 'stimulate abdominal muscle recovery', but really they are just overpriced bike pants. Spanx on crack. At a premium. And on that sticky summer day, as you try to wrestle them on over the giant maternity pad crammed between your legs, it feels a little like being swallowed whole by a boa constrictor.

You shelled out 250 bucks for that pair on the way home from the hospital, in the hope they'd magically shrink your saggy belly and wobbly thighs back to pre-baby shape. Talk about priorities. You've just given birth to a healthy baby boy, but not even the warm love bubble of new motherhood can protect from the gnawing desire to 'snap back', Kardashian-style, to your pre-baby body.

Everyone feels that inescapable body pressure, but you got an extra-enormous dose of it. You'll be back at work hosting a morning TV show under the gaze of the entire country in a few short months. Not to mention running the gauntlet of the Logies red carpet in a figure-hugging gown. (Huh. What figure?!?!?!)

So I can understand why the bone-crushing bike pants seemed like a sensible investment. They promised to have you back in your skinny jeans in no time. All you had to do was wear them twenty-four hours a day for three months . . . assuming you could get into them in the first place.

As your perfect son sleeps soundly next to you, you are working on your imperfect body. You're like some sort of deranged Bridget Jones–type character, wriggling into her tummy-control knickers. You're huffing and puffing as you stretch them over fluid-filled knees, past a sad deflated stomach, and all the way up to those milk-engorged boobs.

You're doing all of this while trying not to breathe or make any kind of sound, lest you wake the sleeping baby. I imagine this was how Katie Holmes felt when she was forced to endure that silent Scientology birth. You're lying on the bed, gasping for air and stinking of sweat and sour milk. Suddenly you're overcome with the urge to cry. (And pee, for that matter.)

Seriously, Sarah, what are you thinking?

Okay, so it's kind of true that you did not wear pregnancy well. You were less Kate Middleton, tennis ball on twig legs and more . . . Goodyear Blimp. You gained a whopping twenty-five kilos during pregnancy, a third of your body weight as the doctor helpfully pointed out. Granted some of that was actually a baby. A whopping 4.3 kilograms, plus a freakishly large placenta that caused all sorts of excitement in the birthing suite.

Do you remember those doctors and nurses rushing in with their iPhones as if it was a prize prime rib at the cattle pavilion of the Royal Easter Show? Good times. You were probably carrying a couple of litres of fluid too. Your face and feet swelled to comical proportions. You had cankles. Towards the end of the pregnancy you had to sticky tape your shoes to your legs just to make them fit.

But there's no explaining away the other fifteen kilograms so easily. Truth be told, you gained those simply by eating ALL OF THE THINGS. You couldn't help it. The first three months of pregnancy felt like battling a hangover born of a thousand tequilas. As with any hangover, food was the only cure. Toast was devoured by the loaf. Carbs were your greatest of friends.

By the second trimester, nausea gave way to a ravenous hunger. You always felt starving. You'd roll your eyes at impossibly gorgeous Hollywood celebrities like Gwyneth Paltrow, who smugly confessed they'd battled cravings of 'crunchy apples and spring water'. You could have eaten Gwyneth herself, with the right seasoning and a side of potatoes.

Let's be honest though, Sarah. What brought you here today, to the bed and the fat-sucking torture tights, wasn't just pregnancy. You've always had an uneasy relationship with your body.

It began at nine years old, after a dance teacher said you were too fat to perform in the front row. Humiliated and heartbroken, you were promptly put on a strict diet to shed the totally normal puppy fat of a fifth grader. That incident began a long journey of calorie counting, yo-yo dieting, and – at its worst point – throwing up food. It's hard to remember a time when your self-worth hasn't been influenced by numbers on a scale. The smaller the number, the more you liked yourself.

So falling pregnant was confronting to say the least.

You reckon television puts on ten pounds? Try being pregnant on television. A few months earlier, you'd told the usual horde of media body shamers to 'Get stuffed' on national telly after being snapped looking 'fat and frumpy' (or what otherwise sane people would call pregnant).

People in television who have been doing this for years can apparently hear the snap of a paparazzi camera before they even see them. You don't have that level of awareness. On the day you were snapped, you were completely oblivious to the fact that you were even being followed. You were oblivious to being a celebrity.

It left you hella confused. Why on earth would anyone be interested in the mundane life of a morning TV show host? Well, apparently even the baby bumps of quasi-celebs make for great click bait. And there is nothing an audience loves more than a before-and-after comparison shot that *isn't* flattering.

You were perfect tabloid body shaming fodder. First came the 'Click! Click! Click!' Then came the 'Judge! Judge! Judge!' When the photos surfaced online you were really upset. And then you read the comments. 'Fat', 'disgusting', 'ugly' and 'whale' were just a few of the adjectives thrown around by nameless, faceless internet trolls. It was a cesspool of online hate. You were like a pregnancy piñata who everyone wanted to have a big old whack at.

Former *Sale of the Century* host Nicky Buckley recalled on your show how she copped vitriolic abuse in the nineties for daring to be pregnant on TV. It was two decades before social media, so she'd been trolled . . . by fax. Amazing how they always find a way.

And while these days baby bumps are more common on television, you struggled with your constantly changing body. Every morning you'd sit on a couch surrounded by half-a-dozen cameras. Sometimes you'd catch a glimpse of yourself on the monitor and cringe. Reckon the faceless bullies on the internet were cruel? Ha! The most vicious tormentor was housed in your own head.

Then one day, somewhere in the middle of it all, the self-loathing . . . stopped. Maybe it was just the happy hormones, but you finally started to like your body, possibly for the first time ever. Your body had a purpose, a purpose other than to wear skinny jeans: it was growing a human. Never mind what the scales said, you were busy making elbows, ears, fingers and toes. Hell, you were casually making brain matter while reading the autocue. BRAIN MATTER. It was mind-bendingly awesome.

You finally felt proud of what your body could do. You marvelled as your belly expanded to accommodate that rapidly growing baby boy. For the first time in your life, there were boobs! Full, round boobs that looked womanly and sexy. Your newly acquired C cup actually did runneth over!

'Bugger it. I'm growing a baby!' you boldly declared on television that one brave day, your voice shaky with righteous rage. 'I'm proud of my body and what it's doing.' The audience cheered and the rant went viral. You accidentally became a poster girl for body acceptance.

Remember when your phone started blowing up with all those texts and tweets from friends and even total strangers, virtually high-fiving you for taking a stand? You became a trending story online under the headline 'PREGNANT TV HOST SLAMS BODY SHAMERS!' and your 'epic takedown' clocked up tens of thousands of views on YouTube. It even caught the attention of Hollywood actress and celebrity mum Zooey Deschanel who'd battled her own body bullies during pregnancy. You were thrilled when she shared your rant with her six million followers on Facebook. *That* was cool.

You felt strong and wise and proud.

Then . . . a little bit angry.

There were tons of women struggling with the same old boring body stuff that you were. What sort of sick society were we living in? When other pregnant women stopped you in the street to thank you for saying so publicly what they couldn't, you hugged them and felt all the emotions: sadness, sympathy, a sense of sisterhood, and a simmering defiance that from now on you would be a good role model and great mother. Stuff the scales.

So how the hell did you end up back here, strangled by a lycra stocking and the same old body bully in your head? How did you go from triumph over self-loathing to once again trying to turn your body into something it isn't?

Seriously, Sarah, what were you thinking?

It's going to be all right. In a few moments time, your wonderful little baby is going to stir. You will see the twitch of his tiny nose and peach fuzz hair and feel that overwhelming rush of love.

Love. It's such a strange word. Four letters, two vowels. It seems too small a word to describe the enormous, ground-shaking emotion you felt from the moment your son was born. Like when the midwife laid him on your chest for the very first time. Your world went from black and white to glorious technicolour as you lay there, skin to skin, breathing in that delicious new baby smell.

For months you'd fantasised about holding your precious little boy, and when the nurses gently tried to take him away to the nursery so you could get some rest, you flatly refused. Instead, you cradled him in your arms for hours and *stared*: at his squished little face, his rosebud lips and his tiny hands and feet that were shaped just like yours. Those first few days he barely cried, but he did make lots of noise . . . squeaking and grunting as he settled into his brand new world, utterly oblivious to the fact that he'd completely rocked yours.

Remember how excited you were to bring him home from hospital? The short car ride home was pretty terrifying. You held your breath over every bump, keeping a fiercely protective grasp on his capsule in the back seat. And when you walked in the door, the house felt different. It felt full and happy. *You* were full and happy. You were complete.

You will look at that baby, shake your head in disbelief that he is yours and suddenly? You'll know what to do with those tights, Sarah. You will dash to the kitchen to grab the scissors, sliding the blade between the material and your skin. Then you will slice and snip and tug until the elastic releases its grasp.

You will breathe again.

The compression tights won't have worked their promised miracle (who would have thought?) but as you look at your boy, you will know that your body has. Your magnificent body has carried, grown and nurtured a baby for forty long hard weeks and it will keep him alive in the weeks to come.

And while your body might never be perfect, at least in that moment it will be free.

Love,
Sarah

Jo Stanley

'All your friends' baby announcement photos are perfect pictures of parental bliss, delirious from a cocktail of adoration, exhaustion and tramadol. But when something goes wrong, the photos don't make it to social media.'

Hey girls,

How are they hanging? That's a rhetorical question, of course. You know all too well that ol' Lefty Boob hangs a good centimetre lower than Ms Right. Also, not sure if you noticed but since turning forty, you've sagged so much that your nipples now point outwards. They look away from each other. It's like they've had a fight and each is looking to hook up with someone else.

I've considered shouting you a boob job, but I feel like that would betray the history that led to you looking exactly as you do. We've been through a lot together, boobs. We've had great rollicking good times and, conversely, some of the deepest heartache I've ever known.

Remember how bad you were at keeping a secret? The biggest

secret that any woman can keep: that she's pregnant. But you can't go from a sensible B cup to enormous gazoongas overnight and not have people talk. And that's exactly what you girls did. In that precious time of secret knowledge and daydreams about baby cuddles and discreet barfing into zip-lock bags, long before I felt ready to make that baby known to the rest of the world, you went from Sporty Spice to Dolly Parton.

Not that I was complaining. Being knocked up was an incredible joy. It had taken a long time for that miracle to happen. Then you ladies gave me the perfect cherries on top of my cream sundaes. I had never had big boobs before and I loved them. I felt fun and gorgeous and womanly and sexy and like I'd been initiated into a secret women's league that I'd never been privy to before. I had two new and really popular best friends. We were the life of the party and the party was at the Playboy Mansion – inhabitants my husband and me!

What a great irony then, that when push came to shove, when it came time for you two to feed a baby, it was an absolute disaster. Where there should have been udders, I had two giant blimps; great advertising and hot air.

Before I get to that disappointment, though, I need to return to the birth, because there is a moment in that day for which I need to thank you girls.

When you're pregnant, you imagine the moment of birth will be messy and painful but joyous and overflowing with crazy loved-up happiness. All your friends' baby announcement photos are perfect pictures of parental bliss, delirious from a cocktail of adoration, exhaustion and tramadol.

But when something goes wrong, the photos don't make it to social media.

Our beautiful Willow, named the moment we saw her heartbeat on the screen, was delivered by emergency caesarean. I remember the relief of knowing that after fifteen hours of failed and excruciating labour, it was going to be over. I remember dead numbness from the waist down and a green surgical screen protecting me from the gory reality. The obstetrician holding my brand new daughter up like a bloody puppet, plucked straight from my tummy. I remember peering, anxiously, through the floaty masks and gowns at a table beyond, as she was wrapped tightly. And then, eyes letterboxed by mask and hat, in extreme close-up in my face, blocking my view of her: a paediatrician I'd never met.

'You should know she has a cleft palate,' he said.

It's not a great tragedy, neither is it a rare occurrence. Babies with cleft palates are born every day. Their face and/or mouth failed to form properly in utero, creating a gap in the upper lip or roof of the mouth. Willow's cleft was comparatively minor, just the roof of the mouth. In Australia we have incredible care and very talented doctors, so these babies are, almost always, healthy and happy.

Willow had worried the doctors while she was developing. Differences in the growth of her heart and brain, and other in-utero signifiers, meant a pregnancy of terrifying uncertainty. The kind of unknown that doctors imply with pauses and unfinished sentences because, despite their years of training and experience, they do not have all the answers.

Throughout the pregnancy, all that doctors could tell us was that if a cleft palate had been added to her constellation of symptoms, we would have reason to think the 'outcome' (do you mean my baby?) would be a very, very bad one. So when this cold stranger told me what the ultrasounds had hidden from us – 'she has a cleft palate' – the simplicity of the sentence belied the devastating weight of the fact.

Perhaps that doctor didn't understand or didn't care, but in his hasty telling he stole a sacred moment from me. Because before I held Willow for the first time, before I could smell her, tell her I loved her, imagine a life of unending possibilities for her and promise to be all she would ever need, before the first contact that was as deep and mysterious as time stretching forward and back and standing still all at once, before all of that – I was afraid.

As I took my baby into my arms, when I should have felt nothing but the purest of loves, I instead felt sadness, fear and panic. My heart fell away from me and, for a split second, my heart fell away from Willow too. I failed her. How could I, her mother, not believe with unwavering certainty in her perfection?

The grief of that moment still catches me, out of nowhere, taking my breath from the pain of it. And for the rest of my life I will feel as though I betrayed my baby. She deserved so much more from me than that.

The next minutes or hours after birth are indistinguishable. People and conversations and medical interactions happened around me, while I sat removed, out of focus, like I was looking up from the bottom of a pool. I felt deadened, until you – my booby friends – jump-started me.

Well, you and an incredibly forward nurse who, before I even knew what was happening, pulled back my hospital gown, held a teaspoon to my left nipple and squeezed like she was trying to pinch it clear off. I had no idea what she was doing and why she wasn't being arrested for it. I was shocked and shitty, but it was a life-saving nipple cripple. Not because of the micro-drop of colostrum she wrung from my body but because the sudden shot of pain roused me like a defibrillator. I felt my heart beat again.

As the sting from that squeeze was still smarting, I turned to Willow beside me and placed my hand on her swaddled tummy to settle her snuffly grizzles. I can still feel the shift in my being, from dead numbness to overwhelming life-giving love, from feeling nothing to feeling motherhood for the first time.

Which brings me back to the recipients of this letter, you, my bone-dry bosom. In your defence, breastfeeding is a dance for two, and your partner, Willow, was never going to learn the moves. For babies born with a cleft palate the mechanics are all wrong.

Babies draw milk from the nipple by creating a vacuum when they suck. Where most babies have a roof of the mouth, Willow had a hole up into the back of her nose. Try as she might, there was no chance of her ever producing the goods but I was determined she would have breastmilk so you poor old Jersey cows were introduced to the breast pump.

It's not how I had imagined spending the first month of my baby's life. Her being cuddled by someone – everyone – else while I looked on from the milk shed. But I knew as much about breastfeeding as I do dairy farming, so I did what I was told and subjected you girls to a rigorous and torturous milk-induction program.

My routine included mechanical suckling, kneading, massaging and weird upside down jiggling, as if the milk had just forgotten which way was out. I tried everything – I had midwives feel me up, I drank Guinness and ate garlic. Yet still no milk.

It was painful, humiliating, exhausting and boring. My nipples looked like walnuts, dry and cracked and raw.

I cried all the time.

I cried when my husband looked at me: 'Look away, I'm hideous!'

I cried when he *didn't* look at me: 'You think I'm hideous, don't you?'

I began to dread the moment I was next hooked up to the machine, like it was some sort of medieval punishment. 'This maiden is charged with the most unnatural of crimes – failing to produce life-giving milk – and lo she shall face the Suction Cups of Hell.'

The last straw came when a male pharmacist suggested I measure my nipple diameter, because perhaps my areolae was too big to fit inside the pump's plastic cone. Like I wasn't just a failure, I was a FREAK! I went home and howled, and then made one of the best decisions of my life.

I gave you girls a break and quit pumping.

I stopped being bullied by the cacophony of voices all telling me if I could only do it *properly*, breastfeeding would work, and listened instead to my instinct that said 'this isn't right'.

In the four weeks following Willow's birth, I'd spent more time with that pump than with my baby. It had sucked away my sense of self and made me feel powerless and like a victim. As I gazed at my baby, I knew that was not how I wanted her to see me – and that was not what I saw in her.

Willows bend but they do not break and my Willow was stronger than anyone had expected. The health concerns first whispered about when I was pregnant developed into varying nightmarish but vague diagnoses. We dutifully shipped ourselves from specialist to specialist and subjected her to test after test. I listened and took copious notes and allowed the experts to build a picture of my daughter in an ever-expanding manila folder that, while crucial to her treatment, bore no relation to the Willow I knew.

Then I would take my baby home to cuddle and kiss, sing to and tickle, and I'd look deep into her eyes and know that whatever I was told by someone else came second to what Willow told me herself. What she told me was that she would do it her own way and that she would be okay.

You remember, dear breasts, how we used to lie on the couch, as you shrunk and returned to your unobtrusive former selves, with precious baby Willow nestling into you? Wrapped in a cosy quilt, skin-on-skin, in a reverie of each other's warmth, I allowed myself to be taught by her strength and calmed by our innate knowledge of each other. In that shared heartbeat, external voices of diagnoses and predictions and expectations and failures and advice and judgement ceased to exist and all that mattered was that I loved her.

In the eight years since, and after numerous surgeries, Willow has grown into a healthy, clever, funny, creative and kind little person, known for her love of food – whoever or whatever produces it.

As for you, girls, you're deflated but happy. I'm grateful that you've remained healthy and my heart beats strong and passionate beneath you.

The miracle of you is that as my child grows, from a tiny baby in my arms to now standing, looking up at me, no matter her size, you adapt to be the perfect nuzzling, snuggling, head-resting height. And, judging by the rate of your elongation, when that is no longer the case I expect I'll be able to shake you out like a hanky to dry her tears.

I have gained so much from our struggles together. I'm stronger. Never again will I ignore my instinct. I know that the answers are always inside me; I need only be still and silent long enough to hear them. Thank you for the part you played in me understanding that and thank you for your role in the making of Willow.

She is the love of my life, and the reason I like who I am.

Jo

Emma Macdonald

'When he arrives, your fears for your career and indifference about children dissolve within seconds. You are a convert who has utterly embraced a new spiritual reverence for motherhood.'

Dear Emma,

Well, this is all rather unexpected, isn't it?

Here you are with a newborn in your arms: a son, no less. You, the hard-nosed, outspoken and cynical newspaper reporter and your husband, Paul, the driven and committed political operative, have managed to create just about the calmest, most glorious baby in the world. It feels like a perverse sort of miracle.

You were terrified as you arrived at hospital this morning. While you can manage the adrenaline rush of a twenty-four-hour news cycle, the combative life of press gallery journalism and the unpredictability of Australian federal politics, you are desperately fearful of becoming a mother. You are afraid of losing control, of change and of not being good at something.

Here you are, about to give yourself over to a child absolutely and completely. You've had literally no practice because you generally avoid holding other people's babies. You don't much like children at all, to be frank. But now he has arrived and your life has changed in one extraordinary instant.

As he was lifted from your body, this child did not cry. He was awake and alert, but he did not make a peep. The nurses wrapped him up and delivered him into your arms and he stared at you for the longest time. You drank him in: those eyes, enormous, blue, somehow knowing, and fringed with eyelashes so long they brushed his eyebrows. The room fell still and silent, filled only with the moment.

'It's always the boys who get the lashes,' one of the nurses chuckled.

Then those lashes flutter closed and he sleeps. You hold him to your chest and breathe him in. Right then, you feel prouder of yourself than at any other stage of your life. You have created something incredible. He is special and you sense that from the beginning. Your worries dissipate in amazement and the most overwhelming tidal wave of love. You know this child. You *know* him and you always have.

As you stare at this perfect sleeping newborn, you will briefly remember the shock at discovering you were pregnant with him. How could there have been a time when you didn't want this with every ounce of your being? That feels impossible now. You feel slightly sick as you remember that day you took the pregnancy test in the shopping centre loos and almost keeled over with fright.

You had just spent the afternoon at the hospital with your beloved mum. She was waging a battle with cancer and you'd watched in alarm as her condition went from stable to desperately ill. You looked after her as best you could until eventually you'd followed the ambulance to the hospital for yet another round of emergency surgery.

It's only when they ran out of hospital beds during your mum's long and slow recovery – and they placed her in the maternity ward – that you stopped and looked around you. It hit you like a punch. What you had assumed was your body's way of dealing with shock and distress was actually something far more profound. You were growing a new human being, a baby of your very own.

You raced to the chemist and, afterwards, stood wide-eyed watching those two dark lines develop, signifying your fate. It's actually kind of funny how someone so supposedly switched-on – a trained observer, a professional chronicler of the human condition – could have been so oblivious to growing another person inside her. You still smile a secret smile every time you walk past those shopping centre loos.

It's not that you hadn't been discussing babies. For months now, you'd been getting nagged by friends and strangers alike about when you would take the leap into motherhood. You were 34-years-old and they were obviously hearing your biological clock tick louder than you were. Your focus was elsewhere. As well as your mother and her illness, there was the hard-fought-for career that you didn't want to compromise. Not for anything. Not ever.

In fact, you were more than a little insulted when the topic of babies came up in conversation. When a friend or family member inquired nosily, you'd think to yourself: Wasn't it enough that you were winning Walkleys and writing about issues of national importance? Why were you being measured by the contents of your womb, rather than the contribution you were making to democratic engagement?

The thing is that when he arrives, your fears for your career and indifference about children dissolve within seconds. You have fallen truly, madly, deeply in love. You are a convert who has embraced a new spiritual reverence for motherhood. You decide that you will have more babies and lots of them. You want to fill a house with children and never bother writing a front-page story again.

Those early days and nights are going to be magical and comical in equal measure. The Type-A control freak that you are is going to have to yield completely to the needs of another. You're an only child who is used to forging and forcing her own path in life, but now there is someone else who is utterly reliant on you, robbing you of independence and autonomy.

Prepare for your carefully controlled schedule and curated existence to be shattered by someone who weighs less than four kilograms. You are going to change your attitude to life because there is not really another option. You are going to slow right down, you are going to find joy in the small moments and you are going to utterly delight in this child and all that he can do. You are going to learn to get along together just fine.

Emma, there are going to be tears from both of you because of breastfeeding. Tears galore. Persevere, though, because you will learn this skill without starving your baby. Together you are going to become a team. In those quiet, dark, solitary hours between the dusk and dawn, you are going to think you are invincible.

And then, when the light breaks, you are going to think you are insane, because sleep deprivation does that to a person.

Nothing is going to stretch your physical, mental or spiritual capacities like the exhaustion you are going to experience over the next few weeks. Actually, if we are being completely honest with each other, it will be months at least. Even when he is a toddler, and a child aged three and four and five years old, there will be nights when he is sick and you won't sleep. Truth is that he is more important than sleep. And you're fitting this rather brutal lesson in nice and early.

There are other things that you will learn in these early weeks. That tea can still be comforting even when drunk cold. That you can consume a tin of tuna while standing at the kitchen sink in less time than it takes for him to spit a dummy out. That your husband will still come home to you, and love you, even when you haven't changed your tracksuit bottoms or washed your hair in over a week. You will also learn it is possible to stare at your child for twenty-three of the twenty-four hours in a day yet not tire of his perfection. You will marvel that he wakes up smiling and that his eyelashes are so long they get kinked when he sleeps on them.

Perhaps the most profound joy will come in watching your mother bond with your son. She will stand over his cot to watch his midday nap just to capture that first smile of the afternoon when he opens his eyes and sees her. She will be your saviour when you stumble through her door, hand her the baby and collapse onto her sofa. And when you wake you will smell the delicious meal she has whipped up for you, all while keeping up an endless stream of gentle conversation with her grandson as he watches from her hip.

She will have you in stitches as she covers his eyes while she walks him past a television (she doesn't want him sullied by the daytime TV you've suddenly become partial to), and she will sit in the back seat of your car on the three-hour drive from Canberra to Sydney holding a muslin cloth over his capsule because she fears the sun may taint his perfect skin. No, her arms aren't tired. Well, maybe just a little bit.

You and Paul will often reflect that your mother's and your son's shared gentle natures mean he has more in common with her than his parents. This little boy will give your mother a new lease on life and you will, for two glorious years, imagine that she has beaten this wretched disease.

But, I'm sorry, Emma, she hasn't.

My dear, you must prepare yourself for the hardest goodbye. I want you to know that those last few weeks at the hospice will be as exquisite as they are painful. You will be the constant in her final days as you were in her life. The autumn light bounces off the lake and filters through the trees onto her bedcovers. You will discover that, like childbirth, death is a labour of sorts. It can be long and it is hard.

Your mother will die on a Sunday morning. As she takes her final breath she will open her eyes and look deep into yours and a single tear will roll down her face. She doesn't want to leave you. You will feel a void so great that you can't imagine ever being able to stop crying. The flow is endless. You will go home and collapse on your living room floor and your now two-year-old will climb gingerly into your lap with a face full of concern. It might be hard to believe, but that tiny baby you're holding today will become a walking, talking being who is capable of the most enormous empathy.

He will ask you 'What's wrong, Mama?' and you will explain that you have lost your beautiful mum and that, right now, your heart feels like it is breaking in two. He will place his hands on your chest and lean in to kiss your heart.

And he will help you get through it.

Some days he will be the only reason you get out of bed.

Four years after your son, your daughter will arrive. A girl! A girl! And you will name her after her grandmother and tap into an entirely new well of love and all-encompassing adoration. The first six weeks of this little one's life will be so different to her brother's because, for one thing, she is a different human being. And for another thing, you have at least half a clue of what to do.

Oh, and your career. You'd forgotten about that, hadn't you? You will go back eventually. And you'll be better at it. There will be plenty more front-page splashes, awards and moments of profound pride and satisfaction in what you can achieve as a journalist. You will approach your craft with more wisdom, empathy and knowledge than you did pre-children. Nobody works more efficiently than a woman who has childcare pick-up at 5 p.m.

Emma, even if you did start out as the most accidental and reluctant of mums, you will continue to feel blessed the way you do now. This will be the journey that defines you. Everyone who ever said anything corny about a woman not being fulfilled until she has children is right. Every cliché is spot-on. There are not enough superlatives in the world to chuck at this gift of children.

You are going to love them with all of your heart for all of your years and you will never stop delivering secret and regular messages of thanks to the powers that be for giving you these exact two people. You are still paid to craft words for a living, and that gives you joy too, but at the end of all your days, it's your children's hands you want to hold. Like your own mum, it will be the faces of your children that you want to see as you close your eyes for the last time.

Love,
Emma

Em Rusciano

*'You know the shelf full of baby books in the study? Burn them.
Incinerate every last one.'*

Darling Em,

Well done. Around thirty-six weeks after peeing on a stick in
the one-bedroom flat that you'd been living in for a week with
your boyfriend of four months – and unbeknownst to him, an
expectant father – she's finally here. Just like Mary Poppins, she's
practically perfect in every way.

You heard the nurses. They said they'd never seen such
an attractive newborn! Yes, they probably say that to all the
new mothers, but they looked you in the eye and smiled. The
eyes never lie. Your highly attractive newborn is also a robust
9.5 pounds and has passed all the necessary tests with flying
colours.

That hasn't changed, by the way. She recently received a perfect score on her Year 9 maths exam. This will come as a shock to you, as you well know your brain rejects numbers in all forms. By the by, you still haven't used Pythagoras's Theorem *once* since leaving high school, so your decision to forge Mum's signature to get out of Year 12 trigonometry continues to be a sound one. Well done.

Now. Listen hard, girl. There are a few things I need to pass onto you: knowledge I'm in possession of now at age thirty-eight that I wish you could've had, a newly minted mother, at age twenty-two.

As soon as Marchella was born they whisked her away. She was pulled from you and then taken – at least in your pain-relieving-drug-addled mind – to a far-off land. All you wanted to do was smell her and touch her. You cried silent tears as your body began to heal itself, expelling liquids, blood and happy hormones. But because you were young and inexperienced, you didn't realise you could ask for her to stay with you, to have her lay on your chest and watch her tiny body rising and falling with the rhythm of your breathing.

You didn't know at the time, but you were feeling the first pangs of anxiety that motherhood brings. I'm sorry to say that it only gets worse from here on out. Don't fret, Em, because you made up for that moment with your next child (spoiler alert!). The minute your second baby arrived, you demanded they place her on your chest and leave you alone. Sadly, not having Chella for that first hour still haunts you all these years later.

That was your first lesson as a parent: never be afraid to ask for what you want when your children are involved. Don't let politeness get in the way of what your gut tells you is right. You're the mum.

The first night after Marchella was born was like a vivid dream. They lay her in a plastic tub next to your bed and you didn't sleep at all; you lay awake watching her. She was swaddled tightly in one of the blankets that Nana had the ladies from church make, with her initials embroidered on it. The soft pink fabric was wrapped snuggly around her. The only part of her showing was the perfect tiny face peeking out from the top.

You held your breath every time her eyelids fluttered, alert to any noise or movement she made. It took a while to feel as though she was truly yours. But it happened. You came back from an extremely painful attempt at the first post-birth toilet stop, aka the Dreaded Pineapple Poo. It felt like you were shitting out your internal organs, which some sadistic fuck had covered in knives.

You lay back down in the hospital bed and just as your head hit the pillow, her huge almond-shaped eyes opened. They locked onto yours and you swear that she recognised you. She stared unblinking into your face and didn't make a sound. You lay there, gazing at each other for what felt like hours.

That's the moment you fell in real, proper, life-changing love. The moment you realised what it is to love someone more than yourself. It was a good moment. It's one you go back to even now that she's a teenager, when you tuck her in at night after she's fallen asleep, when she's upset with you, when you're missing her.

I want to tell you that breastfeeding isn't a natural and easy thing to do, despite what the midwives have you believe. I wish present me could be there to reassure you that you are not a failure for finding it so difficult and to not feel badly about the dread you experience before those early feeds.

There was so much pressure and importance placed on you getting the breastfeeding right. Your boobs felt like they might explode at times and you would wake up in puddles of your own milk. Marchella didn't latch on properly for weeks and the cracked and bleeding nipples – that no one warned you about – nearly drove you over the edge.

You could've switched to formula earlier. The crushing guilt over not getting the hang of feeding for an entire month didn't do either of you any good. Believe it or not, you will get there in the end and actually become quite good at the boob meals. You become a speed-demon who could whip those things in and out without anyone batting an eyelid.

Oh, and I'm also very sorry to report that those giant fighter-pilot thumbs masquerading as nipples on your chest are here to stay.

You know the shelf full of baby books in the study?

Burn them. Incinerate every last one.

They'll make you feel like a bad parent before you've even begun. Each night before you go to bed you will worry if you're going to be enough, be a good mother. Don't worry about that: you are.

Also, maybe ease up on the sterilising of everything that comes within a five-metre radius of Marchella. The disinfecting, boiling and sanitising of toys, clothes, bottles, dummies and family members is exhausting you, and exposing her to a bit of dirt every now and then is really okay. By the time your second child rolls out, you're taking the dummy out of the dog's mouth, wiping it on your jumper and shoving it in baby without a care in the world.

I'm guessing you're pretty tired, hey?

Well, I hate to break it to you, old self, but your beautiful baby is nearly sixteen years old now and she still can't sleep. She doesn't like going to sleep, she fights it like crazy, and this is something that you are now finding out the hard way during the first six weeks of her existence. You'll feel like it's your fault or that you're doing something wrong, but it's not your fault.

It's hers. She's an evil cunt.

Not really, she's just a baby . . . but you will mouth that word at her more than a few times. (Subtly.)

Over the coming months, you will try so many things to get her to sleep. You will drive endless laps of the block, so much so that you've been put on a Neighbourhood Watch list. You will fantasise about inventing an extended arm that can both pat and rock the baby, while you are in another room getting shit done. I assure you, the carpet burn you obtain on your elbows and knees from commando crawling out of her room once she has finally fallen asleep will eventually fade. Although the emotional scars of living with a sleepless baby will not. (Okay, fine, they will. We both know I'm dramatic and prefer to exaggerate for effect.)

Sometime soon – when you are at the end of your rope and desperate – you're going to call a sleep school run by well-meaning nuns. The idea is that because they are closer to God, they possess the secret knowledge to unlock baby sleep. Other mothers will whisper about the nuns in hushed tones. You will picture their domain as if it were Narnia meets Bethlehem meets Maria Von Trapp arriving at the abbey.

But babes? It will be a colossal waste of time.

Those cold-hearted sassy nun bitches will try to make you let your baby cry herself to sleep. You know what it's like to cry yourself to sleep and so there is no way you're putting your baby through that. And so, as if it were some sort of meaningful consolation for exhaustion, the nuns promise to pray for you. Sixteen years later, it hasn't worked but bless them for trying.

By the way, darling Em, and speaking of dramatic announce-
ments – soon you will learn the worst, most traumatic, horrific
thing about giving birth, and you *will* be scarred for life. Believe it
or not, the worst thing is *not* that all-too-recent moment of
shitting yourself while making drilling, unbreaking eye contact with
the love of your life, halfway through pushing a turkey out of
your special place. Oh no. The worst thing about giving birth is
going to mothers' group.

In a matter of days, the hospital and your local health care
centre will group you together with other women in your area.
The only two things you will have in common with these women
is your geographical location and that something traumatic has
recently happened to your genitals. You will be expected to sit
around in a circle with your fellow new mothers and passive-
aggressively compete.

*What's that? Jasper is eating solids already? Oh, yes, he's very
advanced. I remember when Noah did that for the first time . . . Three
weeks ago. YOUR MOVE, BITCH.*

Em, there's one more thing we need to discuss and that's the
father of your child. When you told him you were pregnant, he
was less than thrilled and wasn't even sure if he could assume
the responsibilities of a father. You spent a lot of your pregnancy
terrified that he was going to leave. But as you now know, the
second he held that little baby girl, it was game on for Scotty B
and being a dad.

During the first few weeks he alternated between besot-
ted and bewildered. He's since become the father you always
knew he would be. So remember to cut him some slack. Maybe
ease up on the daily crying. You have to let him parent his way.
Let him be his version of a dad and not your version of a dad.

Let's face it, we both know that no one will live up to your old man Vincie Rusciano.

Scotty is doing his best with the tools he has and he develops his parenting skillset every day. He even knows how to braid hair now. He is a wonderful father.

Here in the future, Marchella is about to turn sixteen and she is an exemplary human. She is even choosing to forego Christmas this year so she can travel to Guatemala and build schools for disadvantaged children. I mean, honestly. If we weren't actually physically present at the birth, I would question whether we were actually her mother.

She's smart, kind, strong, confident, and moody as fuck. (On reflection, she's definitely our baby.) She's also one of your best mates. And your other daughter is just as awesome although in completely opposite ways. You sit together and watch *RuPaul's Drag Race* daily. It's the best. You will be so constantly terrified about fucking those children up but so far so good. Everyone is doing just fine.

What I'm trying to say is: you're a really good mother.

Lots of love from the sparkly future,
Em

P.S. Go out right now and buy the trademarks for 'iPhone', 'Facebook', 'Masterchef' and 'Fidget Spinners' – just as a nice impulse buy. Good girl.

P.P.S. This may seem totally crazy, but you know that idiotic rich guy with the bad toupee who owns the Miss Universe Pageant? Put every dollar you have on him being the President of the United States one day.

P.P.P.S. I know, I know. Just trust me. Do it right now. Every dollar you can find, even the ones down the back of the couch. The financial payout you'll receive will be the only silver lining.

Erin O'Neill

'All those years you would daydream about "motherhood" and now it's here and sitting at home with a baby is empty and lonely.'

Dear beautiful naïve postpartum Erin,

You just have to make it to Christmas. That's the mantra that will carry you through this, the first six weeks of your son's life.

I'm going to give away the story's happy ending now, because I can sense you need to hear it: Christmas does come. In fact, as I write this letter Christmas is about to come and go for the third time in Frank's life.

This year there is no trepidation or fear or anxiety like there was in those first six weeks. There is no underlying panic, only the joyful anticipation of time spent with family and of relaxation.

I know it doesn't feel like it right now, but you will make it to Christmas. That little boy isn't only going to grow up, he is going to thrive. And, Erin, he is stunning. He's so funny. He can count to ten.

Your partner is now your husband and, no, I am not joking. He got down on one knee and everything. You laughed in his face. Then you cried. Then you said yes.

I know that you're afraid, but you just have to make it to Christmas. After Christmas, you'll emerge from this fog of absolute misery. You'll realise that motherhood can recover from a truly awful beginning. You'll learn that it's okay not to have felt like the day of Frank's birth was the best moment of your life. Once Christmas has come and gone it's all going to be okay.

Labour was horrific. You're allowed to acknowledge that, you really are. It was not normal. It was terrifying. You almost died and so did your son. You fought like a lioness for thirty-six hours, begging your body to do what you had always been told it was built and equipped and prepared to do. You drifted in a chaotic haze of despair and fear, overhearing whispers of 'episiotomy', 'forceps', 'emergency caesarean', 'he's in distress' and 'prep NICU'.

Eventually those whispers became demands. There were pleas from the women guiding you through. 'You need to get this baby out!' they instructed. On the brink of what you genuinely believed was death, you grasped at something deep inside you, something primal. You pushed with everything you had left. If you were going to die, your last act on this earth would be to get this baby out.

And there he was.

And then? He was gone.

Whisked away by the paediatric team who quickly worked to bring his stats up and help him to breathe. Those miracle workers turned him from blue to beautiful rosy pink.

While the obstetrician dutifully stitched up the horror that had once been your vagina, you felt the first deep wave of it: guilt, tinged with fear. Those feelings lessen with time, although I suspect they'll linger in some form for the rest of your life.

Guilt, tinged with fear.

Welcome to motherhood, Erin.

You heard your newborn scream in pain as his sinuses were flushed. Your rational mind knows he'll never remember that, but the sound still haunts you in the weeks to come. It becomes a tangible signal that, regardless of anyone's reassurances, your body didn't work the way it was supposed to. Your body caused him pain.

When Frank is returned, you gaze into each other's eyes. He lifts his head (which is ridiculous for a newborn) and you're sure as sure can be that he is looking back at you. You're so overcome by love and amazement for this little wonder child that you make a promise to be the best mother you can possibly be.

That night you felt peace for the first time in three days. There is a pure rush of love that is stronger than anything you've ever felt before. You feel a connection to this baby, to this new life, in a way that feels real, not trite or fake. There is a glimmer of hopefulness, which you were worried you'd never feel again. It's small, but it's there.

Sadly, it doesn't take long for your happy anticipation of the future to be overtaken by fear and guilt once more. You learn that your placenta was faulty. That it could have failed at any moment during the pregnancy and you would have lost the baby. You're reminded again that he is a miracle, which in turn creates a deep and sincere dread that you will let him down.

Your feelings and thoughts are a confused mess of hormones and no sleep. You think:

What did I do to deserve him? Will he hate me one day? He's so beautiful. Will he resent me because we don't have much money? Will he love me? I love him so much . . . I think that maybe I don't want to stay at home like I planned. I want to escape. What's wrong with me? Have I made a mistake? Oh God, does this mean I actually don't love him?

You're struggling to understand how you can be so in love and yet so bored by the monotony of it. The first day that your partner and your mother take Frank out of the house, you lie in bed and weep. You weep because you feel such relief. It's a relief to be alone and momentarily free.

You wonder why you can't see yourself walking blissfully through parks, going to mothers' groups and pottering around the house with a toddler. All those years you would daydream about 'motherhood' and now it's here and sitting at home with a baby is empty and lonely. Nothing about this journey is going the way you planned.

You and Liam sleep in shifts. This keeps you sane, but it also means that you never see each other. Your entire waking existence is you and the baby, alone in this small house. Your closest friendship disintegrates within weeks of Frank's birth, never to be repaired, and somehow your loneliness becomes even deeper.

The relentless and difficult process of breastfeeding overwhelms you. You should have known having a baby with an actual giant human man would result in a ferocious feeding machine of a child. You wonder why you didn't think of that when you locked eyes across the room with Liam at that house party all those years ago.

Forty-five minutes on. Forty-five minutes off. Your schedule dictated by the relentless hunger of this tiny infant. You time his feeds, his naps and his shits. Anything to maintain order in the chaos that has become your empty, lonely life. You remind yourself that you just have to get to Christmas and then feel immediately guilty for wishing the time away.

How dare you describe your life as empty? Don't you realise the gift you have been given? Women would give anything to have what you acheived with such little effort. You got drunk and forgot to take the pill; you should be so grateful for what you have. How dare you want to throw it all away?

There are only a few days left before Christmas. You have kept up appearances as best as you can with friends and family. Endless online shopping, Santa photos and quick trips to Kmart for wrapping paper and a little tree have pushed back that sadness and fear. You ordered a customised ornament to celebrate your son's arrival because that's what people do, right?

It's almost here. It will all be better once those presents are opened and the roast comes out of the oven. The anticipation and excitement is dizzying, noxious. You take Frank to celebrate Dutch Christmas Eve with your in-laws and, like every moment of the last six weeks, it doesn't go as planned.

The exhaustion erupts into anger and frustration as you and Liam accuse each other of the worst things imaginable. You are ungrateful. You are a failure. You aren't good enough. You leave promising yourself that the next morning will be different.

You wake up on Christmas Day and the baby and Liam are sleeping. Despite all the build-up inside your head, you don't feel different. You still feel sad and afraid and guilty. You go upstairs to see that bare tree with the smattering of presents beneath it. You wait. You wonder when it's going to feel different. You only had to get to Christmas after all . . .

You go back to bed and watch the dawn through a crack in the curtain before you eventually hear that familiar squawk from the bassinet. It's his first Christmas. You've dreamt of this day for as long as you can remember. Although in those daydreams about motherhood and family life, you always had a pine tree and family were swarming everywhere. This year the tree is plastic, small and grey. It's just the three of you.

Determined to be positive, you kick Liam awake and rush upstairs to the baby. 'Look, Frankie! It's Christmas!' you say cheerfully. The chaos of present-opening begins and still you feel unsatisfied. Why doesn't this feel right? All the presents are gone now and you still feel empty. So empty.

You turn to Liam and ask, 'Hey, where's mine hidden?'

'I'm so sorry. Erin, I'm sorry.' His face falls. 'I didn't get you anything. I forgot.'

You begin to cry. The pain, the fear, the guilt, exhaustion and stress of those six weeks pours out of you in liquid form, an unstoppable force on this most sacred of days. You made it to Christmas and nothing had changed after all.

It will be like this forever, you think despondently. Why hadn't anyone warned you?

Erin, Erin, Erin. It won't be like this forever.

Soon Liam raises the possibility that maybe he could delay going back to work. Maybe he won't go back at all. So you return to study full-time when Frank is three months old. You feel guilty but then you deal with it and move on. You can't pump properly and have to stop breastfeeding at five months. You grieve that one hard but, again, you move on.

You'll go back to work part-time when Frank is nine months old. They will question you, asking, 'Who's going to look after your baby? How are you going to cope?' But by this time you are so confident. You answer truthfully. 'His father will take care of him. And I'll be fine.'

And you know what? You are.

Motherhood will never be easy for you. Your anxiety and depression come and go, but you learn to juggle that just as you juggle everything else. You excel at university against enormous odds and take every opportunity life throws at you. You are brave and unyielding and you become a fabulous mother, whose son adores her.

He loves you so much, Erin. If throwing yourself onto the floor to lament your mother leaving the lounge room to get a pair of socks is love? Well, that golden-haired monster is sick with it. You haven't been to the toilet alone for three months, such is his desire to be always close to you.

Believe it or not, one day you will begin to look back at those early weeks with nostalgia. The pain will begin to ease.

Now, if you don't mind, I will finish here. I have a TV and a handsome man waiting for me. Our son has a regular bed-time now and sleeps through the night (remember sleep?), which means I have two more hours of freedom before bed.

Tomorrow comes with mixed emotions. It is a chance to celebrate and reflect on not only the miracle that is my baby, but the miracle that is my journey into motherhood. Its beginnings were pretty rocky. I'm so sorry you didn't have this letter when you really needed it, but perhaps now someone else will. Besides, you found your own way eventually. Like you always have.

I love you.

Erin x

Janine Shepherd

'It wasn't long ago that you were lying in another hospital bed. Paralysed in the spinal ward, you overhead the doctors telling your dad that, given the extent of your injuries, you would likely never have children.'

Dear Former Me,

You survived: a tragic accident. A near-death experience. A broken body. And now childbirth.

You know, more than anyone, how remarkable that is. What an extraordinary gift it is. As you lie in your hospital bed – your little bundle of joy swaddled tightly in her blanket, cradled in your arms – your heart is bursting with joy and gratitude.

Tears stream down your face and you know with certainty that your internal world has shifted irrevocably. Savour this memory, because in years to come, when things seem overwhelming, it will anchor you to what is truly important in your life.

Becoming a mother will give you a deep sense of purpose. It will take you out of your personal, painful story and into a much larger one. Your own problems will seem insignificant, because you now have greater concerns and responsibilities. It's now your job to help shape this little person to become a valuable member of society and to fulfil her potential.

Believe me, she will blossom and shine and you will feel a deep sense of contentment for how you have managed this new role of 'mum'. The contentment comes not just from 'what' she achieves with her life but for 'who' she is. Along the way she will inspire you to be the best version of yourself.

Motherhood will delight, surprise, frustrate, confuse, amuse, anger and test you, but mostly it will nourish and sustain you. It will teach you the value of selflessness, of unconditional love. It will heal your wounded heart as well as strengthen your mind and spirit. Savour every moment because it will be over not in years but in what seems like a fraction of a second. And you will look back with lament if you're anything less than present for the whole experience.

It wasn't long ago that you were lying in another hospital bed. Paralysed in the spinal ward, you overhead the doctors telling your dad that, given the extent of your injuries, you would likely never have children. He was devastated on your behalf but that was the least of your concerns at the time. You had more important things to deal with then and more pressing questions to answer.

Will I walk again? Will I ski again?

Is my life as an athlete over? And if it is, what will I do with my time?

There were also the more personal, intimate questions. The questions you were once afraid and uncomfortable to ask out loud, in front of other people.

Will I regain feeling in my lower body? Will I regain bladder and bowel function?

Time – and the perspective it provides – is a great teacher. So let me remind you of just how far you have come and how much your eyes were opened to another way of 'being' in this world after your accident. The same way your eyes will be opened to another way of 'being' after becoming a mother.

Back then you couldn't grasp the full extent of your injuries; that the complications of your spinal cord injury would be your constant companions. You will use a catheter for the rest of your life. Urinary tract infections, medications and the like are a regular part of your life and the bane of your existence. The same will be true of bowel problems and the combination will heighten the physical challenges of your pregnancy.

Janine, you will face these issues with the resolve and determination learned as a former competitive athlete. You once believed your body was your strength. It was 'who' you were. It defined you. So losing that presented the greatest spiritual challenge of your life.

You were heartbroken and humiliated on the day you sat in your wheelchair while that doctor – the male medical lummox, as you later described him – forced you to listen to the most dismal outlook for your future sex life. You were horrified as he told you that the spinal cord injury would affect your ability to feel pleasure ever again. Was nothing sacred? What more could you lose?

In that moment, you were robbed of your sense of womanhood but, Janine, look at you now! You could not feel more deeply connected to the feminine part of yourself. You are a mother.

Despite the doctor's predictions about your chances for pregnancy, you proved them wrong once more. This was an unexpected joy, but, of course, it prompted more questions for a woman living with a permanent disability. Your life, it seems, will always be full of questions.

Will I be able to deliver normally?

Will I feel the urge to push?

How will my patched-together spine stand up to the stresses of pregnancy?

Just like with every other challenge you have faced – overcoming paraplegia and learning to walk, drive, and even fly – you will tackle pregnancy with fierce determination. As expected, during labour, the back pain was intolerable.

'Oh my God,' you thought. 'My back is breaking all over again!'

Looking at the bed where you were to deliver, you were nearly overwhelmed by the struggle to walk even that short distance. You had to push this baby out. You bore down with newfound intensity and gritted your teeth. You summoned determination, closed your eyes and gave one more momentous heave as the pain drained from your body and you felt relief.

You had crossed the finish line with a win. No, it was not the Olympic medal you had once hoped for. It was something far greater than that.

There she was. Slimy, bawling and more beautiful than you could ever have imagined. Through the blur of your tears, you knew she was extraordinary. You chose a name that will prove to suit her perfectly: Annabel. And in a few short years, Annabel will be joined by siblings Charlotte and Angus. They will be equally loved and adored.

You will watch on with wonder and delight as Annabel learns to walk, like you did not long ago. She will stumble many times, but she will continue to pull herself up. She will keep putting one foot in front of the other. You will admire her resilience, her tenacity, her spirit and her grit. She's like her mum.

This won't be the only time she falls. Many times over her life, your daughter will stumble and crash, and you will be tempted to wrap her up, protect her from harm always. Resist the temptation. Those experiences will strengthen her just as they did you. Encourage her free and adventurous spirit and loosen your grip, so that she may navigate the world independently, with a sense of curiosity and abandon.

Finally, Janine, perhaps the most surprising part of your journey into motherhood is the great respect you will now have for your body and what it is capable of. Your body may have once been broken and you may have cursed it with everything you had. However, that broken body performed magnificently in creating and delivering Annabel, and you should celebrate that wholeheartedly. You should be proud.

Your strength has nothing to do with your physical body. Real strength doesn't come from something that can be lost. Authentic strength originates from somewhere much deeper. It shines from the defiant human spirit that lives in us all. That quality is what will guide and support you on this journey through motherhood.

Knowing this, and recognising this, is the true gift.

With love,
Janine

Carla Gee

'It's my fight, my purpose to be "here". To be unashamed and visible as a mother and a proud Chinese-Australian woman, and to give my children the confidence that they, too, belong.'

Dear Carla,

'How to Deal With a Postnatal Racial Identity Crisis' isn't a chapter in *What to Expect When You're Expecting* but, oh, how I wish it had been.

The birth of my children attracted strangers who were curious to know: how did a nice Chinese girl like me end up in this private hospital, the birthplace of heirs to white, ol' money dynasties? Race is the surprising and taboo topic that came to define my experience as a new mum. Like an ill-fitting hospital gown, racism has been the stained garment covering my life that I've never been able to remove. But now it cloaked my children as well.

Carla, what I'm going to tell you is a true story.

It's the tale of how my Chinese ethnicity distracted the health professionals I encountered and near-eclipsed the existence of my newborn son. I was a living piece of Chinoiserie who inspired hospital staff to sing this refrain: 'Where are you from?' The answer ('Australia') never satisfied them because the questions kept on coming. Why was my English so good? And why didn't my children *look* Asian? Who is their father?

For unbelievers, these sort of awkward racial encounters are about as serious as an English drawing-room comedy. They are full of misunderstandings and folly. Ever keen to placate, the racism sceptics will say: *'They have a good heart. Maybe they needed to know for a medical reason. Your hormones are making you too sensitive. You're sleep-deprived and emotional. They couldn't have meant that!'*

People who speak like this probably had their brain abandoned in a handbag at Victoria Station, like in a zombie version of *The Importance of Being Earnest.* People who speak like this don't get it. Or don't *want* to get it. They don't want to believe that this kind of prejudice is real.

I got it, because I lived it.

And it was real. It is always real.

The posh hospital where your son is born will start to feel like an extended episode of *Who Do You Think You Are?* with never-before-seen footage and a blooper reel. The staff are obsessed with your genealogy. They insist on knowing where you, your parents and grandparents were born.

Much to their frustration, your answers aren't straightforward. You're ethnically Chinese, but neither you nor your parents were born in China. Yes, you identify as Chinese, but it's hard to feel connected to a place you've never been and to a language you don't understand.

But now that you have two children who are half Chinese and half Anglo-Australian, you want your answers to be better for their sake. You want your Asian identity to have substance – to be something beyond Chinese New Year and chopsticks.

It's hard to answer big questions when you really just want your catheter and urine bag removed, your baby keeps making weird shaky movements with her arms (is that normal?) and you're stressing that maybe you forgot to tick 'ice cream' on your dinner order.

After your caesarean, you're given six days to recover in hospital. That means six days of fixating upon your gorgeous son, Will. You stare at him until your eyes prickle and burn. Is it the light or has his skin turned a deep yellow colour? Yellow skin is the hallmark of jaundice. You're hyper-vigilant because your daughter Emmy had jaundice and spent several days in intensive care, while you secretly cried in your room.

'Does Will look a bit yellow?' you ask the young nursing student who is taking your blood pressure.

'Well, it's hard to tell,' she muses. 'Your skin is kind of yellow, too. People of your, ah, culture tend to naturally have a yellow tone to their skin,' she finishes off with a mumble.

As you're walking through the halls, trying to exercise your legs, you overhear a nurse's conversation.

'I don't know how you tell with these dark girls, Doctor Elliot,' she mutters into the phone. 'How can you see if they have skin discolouration when their skin is already dark? How do you tell, with these girls?'

You walk a bit faster, even though it hurts.

You have a favourite nurse, Maggie. She's efficient, grandmotherly and makes you feel like you're her only patient even though the ward is full.

'I'm worried that Will's skin looks yellow and that he might have jaundice,' you confide in Maggie.

'Well, you're pretty yellow yourself, aren't you, love? You don't mind me saying that, do you?' she says, with a wink and a squeeze of your arm.

You laugh a little too loudly. It's the sort of laugh that shrieks through a barbeque, as the snags are sizzling and tins of beer chill in an esky. You avoid Maggie's eyes and look at your son instead. Later, test results will show that Will doesn't have jaundice. An additional result is that you don't have a favourite nurse any more.

At the fancy hospital you can leave your newborn baby in an overnight nursery, where the night nurse, Judy, takes care of him. As you gratefully collect Will early one morning, Judy is keen to chat about her weekend. It feels good to listen, because it's like having a friend in this impersonal place.

Judy excitedly tells you that her daughter took her to a special movie night where there were free gift bags. She finds the pink polyester tote and begins rifling through it. There's a bunch of stuff in there – pamphlets, moisturiser sachets, a crappy-looking scarf.

'Can I give you these soy sauce and oyster sauce samples? You probably cook with them, don't you? I can't have them because MSG makes me sick.'

You smile for a bit too long, and it occurs to you that you should take them and thank her. Back in your room, you squash the sauce samples into the sides of your suitcase, deep down so that nobody can see them.

The next morning, you collect your son from his final nursery stay. Judy seems flustered and tense as twenty babies sob loudly in unison. You don't stop to chat this time because she looks so busy. You sign baby Will out and start to wheel his bassinet away.

'STOP!' Judy screams at you.

You turn around, startled.

Judy lunges towards you and snatches the wheeled cot out of your hands. She points to the name card above Will's little head, gets right up in your face, and hisses.

'The surname there is Gee! You're not Gee!'

Oh shit, you realise. *She thinks I'm trying to steal a baby. She thinks this white-looking baby with the Anglo surname isn't mine because I'm Chinese.*

Yesterday, while gazing into your son's face, you and your husband had playfully tried to decide whether Will looked more Chinese or Anglo-Saxon. Or is he the perfect mix of the both of you? It's moments like this, when it appears you're kidnapping a miscellaneous white baby, that the answer becomes obvious. Your baby doesn't look like he belongs to you.

Judy is looking at you like you're a stranger. That's when you realise that she's not your special friend – instead she's someone who likes to natter on about her life to everyone she encounters. Just because she gave you Chinese sauce doesn't mean that she remembers you.

You grimly press your lips together and hold out your arm for Judy to read your plastic hospital ID bracelet. An expression of undisguised horror comes over her face. She apologises and apologises, and is still gabbling repentantly and clutching at your arm as she walks with you to the door and into the corridor.

Back in your room, you are angry, but you feel strangely guilty too. It's as though you really did steal a baby. Somehow, this feels like your fault.

Sheryl from the local baby health centre has phoned to arrange a complimentary home visit from a nurse. You're absent-mindedly answering questions about your address and date of birth as you attempt to quieten two-year-old Emmy and breastfeed baby Will at the same time. An unexpected question snaps you out of this motherly haze.

'Any cultural issues?' asks Sheryl casually.

You honestly have no idea what she means, because sometimes when you hear the word 'culture', you think of ballet and art museums.

'What do you mean by "cultural issues"?'

'Well, some Asians make you take your shoes off before you go in their house, so we bring foot coverings if we know in advance,' she replies helpfully.

You explain that while you are Chinese, the nurse is welcome to wear shoes in your home. You boldly declare yourself to be free of 'cultural issues'.

A week later you open the door to the community nurse, Laura. She pulls from her handbag what appears to be two blue shower caps, and proceeds to shove them over her boots. For some reason you thought the shoe coverings would look a little more chic.

You tell Laura that she can wear her shoes in your house. She is confused and insists on the shower caps. You repeat that she doesn't need them. Finally, Laura accepts defeat, and the shower caps go back in her bag. She's trying so hard to be considerate. You wish this didn't make you so uncomfortable.

Laura is excited to meet you as there really aren't many Asians in your small bushland suburb. She asks more questions about your Chinese heritage than she does about the baby. She laughs and shakes her head when she hears that you named your son William.

'Does he at least have a Chinese middle name, with a special meaning?' she asks, enthusiastically. 'I just love Chinese characters. They're so beautiful.'

You battle to keep your face a pleasantly smiling mask while your mind generates sarcastic retorts. In this fantasy, you would respond with a killer line: 'You know, I'm a writer, so I wanted to name my son after a poet. We named him William, after William Shakespeare. But now that you mention it, of all the poets' names I considered, Confucius wasn't one of them.'

You immediately feel guilty for having nasty thoughts about this caring community nurse. What the hell is wrong with you? She's just being curious and respectful. Why does this irritate you so much? Could your racism radar have been a bit over-sensitive, a bit . . . *off*? Is this what 'baby brain' looks like – a big, extended 'duh' when it comes to race relations?

If only there was a way to prevent these cringe-worthy moments, something like an anti-racism vaccine. You're obsessed with vaccines at the moment, thanks to your newfound paranoia of dangerous diseases. The day you took Emmy home, every person walking through the hospital resembled a gigantic, disgusting whooping cough germ. You hurried to avoid them.

You've come up with a solution. You will keep your babies at home for six weeks straight, and ban any unvaccinated visitors. You will not take them outside for anything – not even a walk – until the day of their first vaccinations. You don't tell people the real reason for this hermit-like behaviour, for fear of looking crazy. So, instead, you offer the kind of excuse that everyone loves.

'It's because I'm Chinese,' you declare. 'It's a Chinese tradition that is very special to me and that I want to honour.'

According to Chinese friends and family, Chinese mothers and babies traditionally do not leave the house for the first month of the baby's life. To you, this custom is conveniently similar to your self-imposed quarantine, plus it sounds much more socially acceptable and also exotic.

Thank goodness nobody asks you *why* this tradition takes place, because you're not completely sure. You've heard it's something to do with the mother not getting wind on her back and you know there's a 'no hair-washing' rule. But you rarely ask questions about your cultural heritage because it makes you feel dumb.

You want to be better than that for your kids. You want to be the mum who knows and embraces her background. Not some clueless 'banana' who is yellow on the outside, white on the inside.

So you feign an ancient understanding, a race memory. For you, the first six weeks of your children's lives are crucial. You want to keep them alive and guard them with everything you have.

But you still want clean hair.

*

Motherhood magnifies the most essential human experiences. For me, nestled among my redefined experiences of sleep, womanhood and family, was my identity as an Australian. As I was constantly reminded that I didn't appear to match or belong in my own country, I became even more adamant that my place was *here*. It's my fight, my purpose to be 'here'. To be unashamed and visible as a mother and a proud Chinese-Australian woman, and to give my children the confidence that they, too, belong.

I want my children to be proud of their Chinese and Australian heritage, but, more importantly, I want them to be proud that they are loved. Asia and Australia may be mighty continents, however, it's my small children who matter to me the most and make me who I am.

They are here, in my heart, and they always will be.

With love,
Carla

Jen Clark

*'No map, no amount of reading or prenatal pilates, no
"best-practice" guidelines, no endlessly flexible set of expectations
or abundant inner self-belief could have possibly equipped you for
navigating the terrain of these first six weeks of caring for a new life.'*

Dear New Mum Jen,

One Sunday morning three years ago, you made a momentous decision. Thinking back now, the day was surreal. You'd had too much sleep, way too much coffee and after years of deliberating, you pressed post on an advertisement offering to donate your eggs to a complete stranger.

It was by far the best decision you ever made. You managed to help a beautiful family have a desperately wanted baby. And one day – to your surprise and delight – they would return the favour. At age thirty-eight, with that family's help, you became pregnant, and now you and your partner, Kirstie, are mothers to baby Max.

Despite your innate penchant for cynicism, it seems that karma might just be real.

Your tale of motherhood is an unusual one; it's back-to-front. It began with the donation of fifteen eggs that when paired with your recipient family's sperm resulted in five high-quality embryos. These embryos were frozen for a couple of months before one was transferred to your recipient mother-to-be.

After more than ten unsuccessful rounds of IVF and one miscarriage, she found out soon after this transfer that she was pregnant. Flash forward nine months and a little baby boy arrived. What a mountain of joy that was.

There were still four embryos left.

When Christmas the following year rolled around, it brought some paperwork with it. You and the couple you'd donated to had to collectively make a decision about the destiny of those embryos. Should they remain frozen indefinitely? Should they be donated to science? Should they be given to another couple longing for a family? Or should they be destroyed?

You discussed it briefly over dinner, but the conversation felt unresolved. Later that night, the recipient father called. He and his partner said that if you and Kirstie wanted to try to have a baby of your own then the four remaining embryos were yours. While you explained you needed time to think it over, your first reaction was elation. There was a huge surge of warmth in your heart. The decision was made.

Early the next year, you began the IVF process in earnest. It was invasive, painful, exhausting and the cause of much heartache. It involved exploratory procedures, eccentric Chinese herbalists and even a short-lived episode of experimental dieting.

The first embryo transfer was extremely painful. You retreated home, wounded but nevertheless hopeful. Ten days later, you woke on the morning of the pregnancy test with abounding excitement, but wracked with anxiety and completely wrung-out from the night's restlessness. You placed all of your hope in the fact your period had not appeared . . .

And then it did.

Fuck your body, fuck everything.

You started sobbing hard, not caring about who saw or heard you. You were absolutely shattered and walked as quickly as you could through the bustling hospital foyer, out the door and to your car. You sat there in the front seat of your car, your elbows resting up against the steering wheel for God only knows how long. Then you drove home, eyes red, weepy and stinging, your heart cracked, your head full of disbelief.

Another month came and went and, with it, you did a lot more research. You had a few big nights out with mates, talked it through, got your shit back together and decided to try again.

Another painful transfer.

Another journey home, wounded and raw. Once again, unsuccessful.

In early July 2016, you were in the throes of renovating a flat and were super-glad to have some distracting physical work to sink yourself into. You'd taken six weeks 'off', and during that time had engaged a different IVF doctor. He was a much friendlier, more approachable chap, known for his accessible demeanour and willingness to take the time to actually answer his patients' questions.

Plans for transfer number three were underway. This time, you ate what you wanted, cooked some healthy but nonetheless comforting meals, worked as per normal (although assembling furniture, scrubbing, sanding and painting walls and hauling bloody heavy boxes of floor tiles across a house on a daily basis were, admittedly, a little on the atypical side). You tried to get a sensible amount of sleep, but this time there was no acupuncture, no fad diets, no magic pills and no woo-woo.

When pregnancy test day came along, you had adopted a firm 'que sera' mentality. Despite your hopes still being high, your feet were firmly planted in reality. You ventured to the hospital amidst the heavy early morning traffic on Punt Road. You arrived, went up to the seventh floor and walked, as nervously as usual but this time with Kirstie by your side, into pathology. You waited. You went in. They drew blood, taped your arm up with cottonwool and you walked out. Sigh.

At a hipster cafe nearby, you and Kirstie sat yourselves up at the bar and savoured your strong skinny cappuccinos while trying to think of anything but pregnancy. The morning dragged while you waited for a call from the nurse. You walked the dog to kill time. It was middle-of-winter-in-Melbourne cold and you were incredibly agitated. Then, finally, there came a text message from an unknown number. *Yay! Levels are looking excellent, Jen. Well done, Chris.*

It was from your new IVF doctor. You turned to Kirstie, beaming. 'Oh my God, I think we're pregnant!'

Max arrived safely in March the next year.

Now, you're pretty much the seasoned professional when it comes to massive change, having lived in over twenty-four houses

in your thirty-nine year lifetime, having had five serious relationships and run two businesses. But no map, no amount of reading
or prenatal pilates, no 'best-practice' guidelines, no endlessly
flexible set of expectations or abundant inner self-belief could
have possibly equipped you for navigating the terrain of these
first few months.

The first week or two of your foray into motherhood is a
continually unfurling, unpredictable reel of challenges. From
the moment of Max's birth, the very second you turned from
one into two beings, your priorities were forever transformed.
It was like learning to walk all over again but this time on stilts,
trying to intuit what this new human needed, when he needed it
and how you could best provide it.

You had to do it all while drawing on what seemed like a per-
petually empty tank of physical and emotional strength. You had
to maintain your nerve around someone so little, so fragile, so
unknowing, so needy, so new. You had to reformat the person
that you were and metamorphosise from Jen the independent
agent – the individual – to Jen the Mum. You had to become
a master anticipator, an astute observer and an efficient and
effective responder.

There were so many voices competing for your attention.
It seemed that nearly everyone had an opinion and that everyone
was right. All you wanted to do was to love Max in your own way
and in your own time. To hold him and soak him up. To bask in
his smell. To marvel at what would become one of your favourite
pastimes: watching him sleep.

There were nights when you found yourself sitting in the
dimly lit silence of the living room at 3 a.m., staring at the sil-
houettes of the gently rustling trees out in the back courtyard and

desperately trying to rock Max to sleep as he fed on your intensely painful breasts. It was in those moments that the most random black thoughts would enter your mind. *Max will never know you thought that*, you'd assure yourself silently, the tears streaming down your own face and splashing onto his.

For a while you thought you might be on the verge of postnatal depression but, as time progressed, these episodes thankfully waned. You accepted that you were just hardwired for middle-of-the-night, anxiety-riddled introspection, which has always been a thorn in your side.

Four or so months in, things started to change. It didn't become easier but you adjusted to the demands of the new daily routine, a bit like wearing in a new shoe. It fit better and more comfortably. The leather had softened. You accepted that this journey was going to be an erratic one: one that you couldn't possibly predict.

That said, having to return to work within two weeks of Max's birth was undeniably gruelling. Between parenting, running a business and managing ongoing physical pain, there was little space for patience. Your shit-tolerance threshold hit an all-new low. You couldn't be bothered with facades any more. Later, you would realise this was actually a fabulous thing, a revelation of sorts. This parenting gig made you more loyal to *your truth* than any other life event ever had.

And you started to find, interlaced with the frequent experience of complete overwhelm, moments of utter beauty like nothing else you've ever experienced. The sheer delight on Max's face when you greeted him in the morning would often make you well up. The intensity with which he gazed at new objects. The look of amazement on his face when you played him music or sang to him. His willingness to learn and absorb. He was so untouched and unaffected by the world and to you that was beautiful. You just wanted to soak up all of his innocence. Looking back, the machinations of the IVF process and the emotional and physical rollercoaster you went on to bring this so deeply loved, so indescribably and unbelievably cherished new soul into your life seem so distant now and, frankly, so short and trivial. It pales in the face of a new unfolding life.

You keep reminding yourself that no matter what happens to you, or to him, and regardless of how you both evolve as people, what complex challenges life throws at you or circumstances you find yourself in, individually or together, Max will *forever* be a part of you.

And for that, you are nothing but eternally grateful.

Jen

Kirstie Innes-Will

'There's no roadmap for what this kind of parenting looks like and that can be as liberating as it is anxiety-inducing. Unfortunately, 99 per cent of parenting literature is written for birth mothers.'

Dear Kirstie,

You've got this.

It doesn't feel like it in this moment, but you have everything you need to get through this. This is actually the worst part. Waking up with your heart hammering in your chest, after barely an hour's sleep, only to find an empty bed beside you. Unable to sleep, you count the minutes, waiting for the hours to go by until they'll let you back into the maternity ward again.

The dream you just had – in which you return to the hospital to find Jen telling you tearfully 'the baby died' – is just that: a dream. Max, your fierce little angel of a newborn, is doing fine. At the exact moment you woke – yes, right then at 2 a.m. – he was pulling at the wires attached to his chest, tugging at his breathing tubes and disconnecting himself from the machinery of intensive care.

A nurse will check on him and see that his breathing is improving and decide that, actually, she's going to let him be. She will see that he can now breathe unassisted. Slowly but surely he is improving because he is one of the lucky ones. Max is one of the babies who can count their stay in the Neonatal Intensive Care Unit by the hours, rather than days.

The adrenaline that kept you on your feet all day won't loosen its grip for some time. That's a good thing, because you'll need it. These four days while Jen and Max are in the hospital will be exhausting in a way you've never experienced before. Exhausting – and also enraging.

The exhaustion you expected, but the anger takes you by surprise. Right now, you feel angrier than you ever have in your life. That fire serves a purpose. It makes you fight for your little family. First, to reunite Jen and the baby she just gave birth to. To get them back together in the hospital. Second, to bring them home as soon as possible. Home, where they can fall into the deep sleep of relief and familiarity. And third, for the three of you to be acknowledged as a family unit with as much legitimacy as anyone else.

The hospital staff question your status as a family. All day, ad nauseum, it's been: 'Who's the mum?' 'Which one's the mum?' Clearly, the one in the bed, the one with the hospital wristband, is the patient, is the *birth mum.*

But that's not what they mean.

What they mean is: 'Explain why you are two women.'

In the operating theatre, the paediatrician who assessed Max's breathing, apparently baffled by your presence beside the resuscitation table, asked blankly: 'Sorry . . . who are you?' When you explained that you're Jen's partner and Max's mum, the doctor responded with silence.

'I'm not just some random,' you added, in desperation.

You didn't realise what a toll all these micro-aggressions would take.

Some of the anger comes from the powerlessness you felt watching your little family get spun out of the operating theatre and sent in two different directions: Jen to recovery and then up to a ward and Max into a portable humidicrib and then to NICU, two floors down. All day you pinballed back and forth between the two people you love most in the world, not even bothering to take off your surgical scrubs.

You want nothing more than for Jen to be able to hold Max. You need to hang on to that determination, because in a few hours time – in the absence of assistance from the nurses – you'll have to help Jen hobble down to NICU, leaning on your arm. Then Max will feed and, fortified, he'll get cleared to come up on the ward. You'll get your first glimpse of peace together as a family. Your fight will be worth it.

The birth was the most whirlwind of days, starting with the surreal caesarean, where you and Jen felt like secondary characters: an afterthought in the day-to-day business of extracting babies. The next few hours disappeared in a blur of beeping machines, tubes and monitoring, as you watched Max's heaving chest become gradually less distressed. Time seemed to fly, even though your aching feet hinted that hours had passed.

In the midst of the chaos, there were moments when your new status hit home. You signed forms, told the nurses what Max's name was so they could print ID tags, you consented to a dummy. And just like that, you became a mum.

Like most mums, you will find yourself having to defend your parenting decisions in those vulnerable early days. In the maternity ward, the little orange dummy – which gave Max such comfort in NICU and helped convey the colostrum that Jen expressed – will be frowned upon. Both you and Jen will see that it's comforting him and decide to trust your instincts. He'll quietly wean himself off it in a few months time.

This is an early lesson that things have a natural time and place in a child's development. Tuning in to him and seeing the opportunity to let go or move to the next phase when he's ready will help you to navigate things more smoothly.

I know you were unsure what it would be like: to be non-birth-mother (and surely there's got to be a better word for it than that). But those fears are going to melt away in the coming weeks and months. Max may have wrapped his fingers around yours absent-mindedly at first, but he'll soon be gripping them at any opportunity, especially while feeding. He'll stop crying when he hears you sing for the first time. You'll be the one whose silliness prompts his first laugh. Soon you'll share jokes: tricks you play that always make him smile.

Max will feel as intrinsically *yours* as if you had once carried him inside your own body.

There's no roadmap for what this kind of parenting looks like. That can be as liberating as it is anxiety-inducing. For you, it's annoying because you like to read widely on the subject of a new endeavour before embarking on it. Unfortunately, 99 per cent of parenting literature is written for birth mothers – with the odd token mention of a father who is assumed to be working full-time after the first week anyway.

This infuriates or frustrates you, because you're not a father.

You're not the parenting literature model of a father who 'generously' cooks a few dinners, 'minds' the baby occasionally and changes the odd nappy. While you welcome the chance to compare notes with dads, you also differ even from your friends' male partners who share parenting duties close to equally. The truth is that you can't ever be a father, because you bring to parenting all the societal baggage of being a woman, not a man.

Occasionally, this works in your favour. Responses to you taking six weeks initial parental leave are overwhelmingly positive, whereas many men face snide comments or open disbelief in their workplaces when they request the same. But most of the time it's limiting. Society's ideal mother is a vaginal-birthing, breastfeeding, non-working paragon of domesticity. You can't be that and nor can many mothers.

The sooner our world moves away from the notion that there is a single 'correct' form of mothering, the better. Neither you nor Jen are going to live up to that model, but guess what? It doesn't mean that you're not both going to be fabulous parents.

Despite all the preparation, you won't get the chance to breastfeed Max after all.

I'm sorry. Let it go.

You can be proud that you tried to follow the protocol for inducing lactation, which is not easy with a demanding job and domperidone making you jittery. Breastfeeding isn't as essential for bonding as it is so often made out to be. You'll discover that combination feeding is the right choice for your family and leads to a happy, thriving, rapidly growing little fellow who takes bottle or boob at will.

This will allow you and Jen to share night feeds and to be slightly more mobile (pop a bottle in the bag and head out!).

Friends will later confess that they wish they'd introduced a bottle earlier so they didn't end up in a spiral of isolated exhaustion when, six months in, they're still the only one able to feed their child because he or she is now old enough to refuse a bottle.

There will be a lot of these moments – where the right choice for your family runs against the dominant paradigm. You'll get calmer and more comfortable with that. In fact, parenting will make you much more self-assured. For years, you've worried about how you would cope with the immense responsibility of raising a small person in a world which bombards parents with dramatically contradictory advice.

But now that you're finally a mum, you're rapidly developing a thick skin.

You'll use your own critical judgement, find reliable, non-biased information, do your own research into evidence bases when you need to and, above all, you'll tune in to your baby. So much of parenting is trial and error *with your specific child*. Observe him as closely as you can and he'll show you the way, this fierce little baby who emerged out of the womb fist raised.

When he cries (and, yes, he will cry a lot in these first weeks) try a new jiggle, bounce, walk, rock, song. Does he quiet? Or is he still wailing just as hard in a few minutes time? He's still crying? No worries, try something else. There are no magic pills that work for all children. Max, for instance, despises the white noise machine that so many people swear by. Keep trying and be prepared to try something else if one method doesn't work.

Don't get me wrong: these first few weeks will be hard, but they won't be the total nightmare that you feared. There will be so much joy. When you first take him home, especially, you and Jen will be giddily euphoric. The joy will crash into fatigue and break out in stormy tears at times. Don't panic. Just let it wash past.

These first weeks will be very hard on Jen. Breastfeeding is exhausting and she'll still be in a lot of pain. The parenting books would have you believe that during this time your role should be peripheral, confined to providing meals, tending to guests and perhaps changing the odd nappy.

But there are a lot more satisfying parental chores, like organising his teeny clothes into piles so you can grab an outfit easily when changing him, bathing him and dressing him for bed, letting him fall asleep on you. These will help Jen out just as much.

Above all, keep your sense of humour even among all the anger you've been feeling. Don't fall into the earnestness that plagues modern motherhood. Babies are hilarious little creatures. So noisy, so snuffly and emitting so many effortful farts.

Above all, keep fighting. It's worth it!

Kirstie

Bronwyn McCahon

'Don't worry that you feel disconnected from your husband right now. It's normal to be resentful that he gets to sleep in another room banking eight hours of uninterrupted sleep, while you're being woken every twenty minutes by a baby who's acting like she's just been fed acid.'

Dear new-mum me,

It's time. She's out and she's alive . . . So let's get that manky arm cleaned up.

You were only six weeks pregnant when you had a bleed while on a work trip in India. It scared you senseless. So when a magic healing man gave you a 'special stone' to keep the pregnancy safe, it made total sense to keep that stone bandaided to your arm . . . for eight long, sweaty, hormonal months.

Having a rock stuck to your skin with a sticky plastic strip has made your arm a little, um, gross. Also infected. Let's sort that out now, shall we?

On the plus side, it worked. The magic healing man and his stone came through for you. You're mum to a perfect little girl, Harper, and she is the most magnificent – and terrifying – thing you've ever seen.

I know it's hard to believe that Harper is really here after those eighteen desperate months of trying to fall pregnant. The early miscarriage at eight weeks, when you first started trying, made you lose faith in your body and in yourself. You became convinced you weren't capable of making and baking a baby to full term.

But you did it. You did it.

And now we're here. These early new-mum weeks are like being hit by a bus and then reversed over again. Possibly twice. You're going to experience a cocktail of body pains and emotions – both good and bad. This period will push you so far outside your physical and emotional comfort zone that you'll struggle to remember what 'normal' felt like.

You're uncomfortable. She was a big baby and the patchwork quilt your obstetrician stitched down there is making it tricky to sit down (Hint: try sitting side-saddle). That giant mattress-sized pad you've got wedged between your legs is going to remain there for the next few weeks. But at least the extra padding down there will make it comfortable for the hours you'll spend sitting on the couch each day expressing and feeding.

You've got a lot of milk, which is a good problem to have. I just wish you discovered the electric double pump sooner. People keep telling you that you're doing something wrong and the reason you're getting mastitis every second week and eating antibiotics like M&M's is because you're not attaching Harper correctly.

Perhaps what they say is true, but you know what else is true?

Breastfeeding is hard.

Although time-consuming, your solution of expressing every feed and then bottle-feeding the breastmilk is a great one. I'm so proud of you. You could have given up and switched to formula straightaway (which would have been perfectly fine and much easier) but your determination and crazy oversupply of milk has given you, your brother and your best friend freezers full of breastmilk, which will last Harper for the next seven years.

Please stop feeling guilty about the 'lack of connection' by not feeding straight from the breast. And also stop staring at women who pull out a boob and feed so effortlessly while sipping their lattes. I get that you're interested and that they're impressive, but you also look like a creep.

For the next couple of months, it's going to feel like you've lost control of your body. Your milk let-downs are fierce, like someone knifing you in the nipple. Those afterbirth contractions make you feel a tinge nauseated, and stepping out of the shower will be a stressful scramble to pad up the various leaking zones before ruining yet another bath mat.

You're overwhelmed, but those teary moments in the shower when no one is watching are nothing to be embarrassed about. They're actually so important. They're going to do a world of good for your mental and emotional health. Let it all out. Have a good cry about nothing and everything. Then pad up and get back out there, tiger.

I know it may not seem like it, as you sit awkwardly on one butt cheek with frozen cabbage leaves on your enormous boobs, but I'm here to tell you that your body is going to be okay. You will feel healthy and strong and beautiful again. It's just going to take a bit of time.

Right now it feels like your brain is being swallowed up by worry. Worry that she's going to stop breathing. Worry that she's not putting on enough weight. Worry that she's going to get whooping cough and the other 645 diseases you keep googling. It's time to stop now. No really, stop googling. Stop googling.

Harper will get sick. She'll get colds and ear infections, she'll even fall out of her bouncer and donk her head, but eventually all the bumps, rashes and runny noses will disappear and she'll be fine. You all will.

I don't want to pretend that there aren't choppy waters ahead. There will be the moments you will yell at whoever is closest for no other reason than sheer exhaustion. That shrill maniac lady who is lashing out at her husband? Yep, that's you.

Things will get heated and you're going to say stuff to him in anger that even six years later I'm too embarrassed to write down here. Don't worry that you feel disconnected from your husband right now. It's normal to be resentful that he gets to sleep in another room banking eight hours of uninterrupted sleep, while you're being woken every twenty minutes by a baby who's acting like she's just been fed acid.

This is new for all of you and he will adjust the same way that you will. Remember to tell him what you need him to do (dream feeds and every other household chore). And what you don't need him to do (complain about how tired *he* is every morning).

Your marriage is different now – Harper made sure of that. But you married a great man, a man who loves you so very much and who will be by your side through all of this. You'll develop a new and mutual appreciation and the bond between you will actually be stronger than ever. Not every man would go, without a second of hesitation, to the chemist to buy you maternity ~~surfboards~~ pads.

You're exhausted and I hate to be the one to tell you this, but there is no 'magic' way to get Harper to sleep. You think you've cracked it with the white noise, the 7 p.m. bedtime, the copious number of dummies scattered around her cot, hours of bum-patting and the bed tilted on a 20-degree angle, but . . . next week none of that is going to work any more.

You're going to look at her room full of sleep aids and wonder 'What the hell?'

There is no sure-thing formula with this baby. Some nights she'll sleep better than others and some nights will be rough. There's not much you can do to change that. I know it's disheart-ening meeting up with other new mums who chat about the seven-hour stretch of sleep their babies are doing at night. It hurts.

Please take comfort in knowing that when Harper is five months old, you'll find a solution. Her name is Jane. Yep, you'll call in the professionals for help and it will be glorious. Jane will give Harper the gift of sleep and give you your sanity back.

Your head is foggy after another night of micro-naps and you're desperate for answers. Why won't she sleep longer than twenty minutes? Why is she so uncomfortable after each feed? Why is there a blister on my nipple?

And the biggest question of all: Will life ever be the same?

Six years and two more kids later, I can tell you with abso-lute certainty that the answer to that last question is no. Life will never be the same. Not even close. It will be so very different, but also so much better than you can imagine right now.

Your life with three kids is hectic and noisy, but gloriously fulfilling. Waking up every morning at 6 a.m. to Theo standing beside your bed sucking his thumb two centimetres from your face will better than any sleep-in. The way Grace makes a funny little grunting sound at night while you read her bedtime stories will be a sound you look forward to hearing every day. And Harper's passionate – verging-on-suffocating – hugs will be something your body can feel even when you're not with her. You've created awesome little people and your days ahead are filled with so many spectacular adventures.

I know it's hard right now. It does get easier.

And harder. And easier. And then harder again.

Listen to your mum when she says, 'It will pass, darling.' Listen to her not only because she's had five kids and knows what she's talking about but also because it does pass. In fact, it passes all too quickly. Try to surrender to each moment. You're going to have rough days and the best days, but as time passes and you watch this little girl take her first step, start kindy and weave yet another Elsa braid through her blonde hair the love you feel for this tiny human will grow to breathtaking heights you never knew possible.

Bron, you think you love her now, but just you wait.

You're doing so great, Bron. Go easy on yourself and take time to enjoy the little things – like that sashimi you've been eye-sexing for the past nine months. It's all yours, tuck in. I'm so excited for you to see what's coming . . .

Xx Me

P.S. You just spilt coffee down your pants. It's okay, nobody noticed.

Felicity Harley

'Intuition matters and it is real. Listen to it, feel it, act on it. Remember that you know your child better than anyone else, even at just a few weeks old. You know their cries, their feeding habits, their sleeping or lack thereof.'

Dear Felicity,

You will relive – almost weekly – the same conversation with your husband, Tom, that took place in your lounge room. It was 5.50 p.m. on Easter Sunday. The mustiness of the rental terrace filled your nostrils (renovating your home with a newborn #crazy), as the dwindling rain dripped from the overflowing gutters.

Your two-year-old son, Jimmy, pulls at your Bonds trackies while you cradle five-week-old Hugo in your arms. He's sleeping soundly. *Is his temperature really that much of a worry?* you and your husband ask yourselves. *Are any doctors even going to be at work on a public holiday?* you wonder aloud. *How far is it to the nearest hospital? Really, he seems fine . . . just hot.*

Shit, now his temperature is up to 39.2 °C.

He's a newborn. This is not good. Should we call an ambulance? Maybe we should call an ambulance? I need to give him a feed. Let's not panic. I'll grab the nappy bag. Stay calm. Stay calm. Stay calm. What about snacks for Jimmy? I am so tired. Let's go!

Intuition is the ability to understand unconscious reasoning. And it is something you never truly understood until that life-defining conversation in the lounge room. Your inner voice was reading the situation. It was telling you – deep in your gut – that something wasn't right with your angelic son. It was telling you to drive to the hospital. Immediately.

Thank God you listened.

Emergency at Sydney Children's Hospital is buzzing. 'It's Easter; it's always busy!' quips the triage nurse as you relay his birthdate. You're ushered immediately through the flapping white doors and into your own cubicle while one, two, maybe, three nurses envelop your family in curtains.

The questions keep coming. *Has he been feeding well? Yes! Has anyone had a cold? Yes! How long has he been sniffling? Um, a few days. Is he sleeping? No! He's a newborn. How many wet nappies in the past twenty-four hours? Six or eight maybe.*

Jimmy is clambering up on the spare hospital bed in the corner. He grabs his monkey backpack and rips it open, fossicking for food. It's dinnertime; he's hungry. Hugo starts to cry. He's hungry. You're constantly touching Hugo's forehead to feel if he is hotter. The nurse takes his temperate. It's 39.5 now. *We've got to get a catheter in,* they announce.

Tom keeps repeating that you'll all be home soon. He doesn't know that's the case. How could he know what is about to happen? Nonetheless, that's exactly what you love about your husband: he's always looking for the positive.

The next few hours are a blur of pinpricks, X-rays for pneumonia and a conga line of people in white coats asking questions and feeling your newborn son's forehead. They're going through a list, ticking off everything it might be. You overhear one doctor say the name of a particularly scary condition. You choose to ignore it. They start antibiotics just in case.

Tom takes Jimmy home at 10 p.m., while you and Hugo are transferred to the infectious diseases ward. You have three nappies left for Hugo and no change of clothes for either of you. You're sharing a room with another mother and her peacefully sleeping baby. Throughout that night you cling to Hugo – never once putting him down in the steel-framed cot that you think resembles a tiny jail cell. You ask the nurse to hold him while you do a wee and remove your contact lenses. He can't be left alone. You feed whenever he wants it. You don't care about routine any more. Not in this place.

By 9 a.m., you're moved to an isolation room. There are so many windows that it makes you feel uneasy, vulnerable. Visitors have to wear special suits before they enter. It all resembles a scene from that movie *Contagion*, which makes sense, because the most horrific forty-eight hours of your life are like a scripted Hollywood nightmare.

The doctor orders a lumbar puncture at 11 a.m. because Hugo's temperature isn't responding to the usual methods. Forty degrees is his teeny, tiny new normal. You can't watch it happen. The nurses will comfort him, you think. Some things are better left unseen by the eyes of a mother. Tom goes with him and you are so grateful.

Hugo returns pale and listless. *Almost lifeless*, you think to yourself. You scan his face, his eyes, his skin and his hands for any sign of health. You cuddle him even closer.

Your mum and dad arrive around 3 p.m. and take Jimmy home. He's only two and he needs to be taken away from all the germs, away from all the sickness, away from the infections and away from his baby brother.

The doctor returns with notes from the spinal tap and you're sweating. There's a high white blood cell count in Hugo's cerebro-spinal fluid that indicates his body is fighting a severe infection, probably bacterial. They won't know which type for another forty-eight hours until the lab grows a culture. You hang on every word the doctor says, but all you're hearing is 'bacterial mening-itis' again and again and again. You're terrified.

Felicity, you have everything going for you – a beautiful son, a doting husband, the perfect family, your (in progress) dream house and a successful career. This sort of horror isn't supposed to happen to you. It's supposed to happen to other people but not to you. Right?

Hugo, in his light blue singlet, nappy and catheter that is nearly the size of his arm, is nestled into your chest. He seems so peaceful, so unaware and yet so sick. *We don't know what we're dealing with yet*, the doctor says gravely.

Your mind goes a million miles an hour and you hammer the doctor with questions about brain damage, disability and even death. She doesn't answer. She doesn't want to give you false hope. She doesn't know.

You stupidly open your phone and type in the web address for *Google*. You're a journalist, so you need to know facts and infor-mation and read other mothers' stories. The internet sends both you and Tom to a very dark, very solemn and extremely scary place. You will stay there for hours.

Here in the hospital there is just so much silence, so much pain. Hugo isn't crying and he's feeding well. The nurse weighs his nappy again and he's passing urine. It is what gives you all hope.

The hospital shower is a plastic box at hand-height that dribbles water like a lukewarm beachside tap. You look up and see the 100s & 1000s–like dots on the rim around the top and try to take your mind to nothingness. You need these showers. You need them to gather your thoughts, to escape the confronting sick children in adjacent rooms and dodge the forlorn parents pacing the dreary halls.

Your hair is dirty, breastmilk drips from your boobs, your stomach still puffy from your C-section. It is the only time you let go of your son. The only time you let go of your precious child who is fighting a hideous disease. The shower is salvation.

Except for the showers, you hold Hugo near constantly for three days and nights. Well, you let go of him just once to catch the lift downstairs to the cafe to drink a chocolate milkshake with Jimmy. You miss Jimmy. He, like everyone who has been in contact with Hugo in the past week, has just had a vaccination. Please God, don't let him get this thing too.

It's Wednesday when you *finally* get confirmation on exactly what Hugo is battling. A touch of pink has returned to his beautiful face. Hope. Four doctors shuffle into your room and you ask for the bad news first.

Hugo has contracted Meningococcal B.

You cry. You sob. You're relieved. You're scared.

The good news is that because you and Tom acted so fast getting him to the hospital and he was given precautionary antibiotics within hours of his temperature spike, you might've saved his life. Hugo will likely recover and without any lasting effects.

You stay another forty-eight hours before being moved into a shared ward, where you try to establish some normalcy.

Aged just over six weeks, Hugo is discharged from hospital for the second time. It is your birthday and it's bittersweet. These events have changed you forever. This shock and pain and panic will be the reason you're forever more present with Jimmy and Hugo. It will help you prioritise your children over *everything* else. It will teach you not to sweat the small stuff. It changes your view on your career, your relationships and your life.

Intuition matters and it is real. Listen to it, feel it, act on it. Remember that you know your child better than anyone else, even at just a few weeks old. You know their cries, their feeding habits, their sleeping or lack thereof.

Felicity, don't second-guess yourself. Trust your gut because your gut knows what's up, and if in doubt always see a doctor. You are not being silly or overcautious. You are being a worried mum and that is perfectly and completely normal. Being worried just saved your boy's life.

Well done and I love you.

Felicity xx

Editor's note: Meningococcal B is the most common form of meningococcus in Australia and is not currently included on the National Immunisation Program Schedule. Hugo's symptoms were drowsiness, irritability and fever. It was his increasing temperature that made Felicity question that something wasn't right. He did not have the infamous purple rash.

The Meningococcal B vaccine is currently available on the private market at a cost of approximately $150 per dose, meaning you have to ask your doctor for it and to administer it. Felicity is hopeful the vaccine will be mandatory in Australia in the future, as it is in New Zealand and the United Kingdom.

Suzannah Bayes-Morton

'The power in your body, its knowledge and its innate intelligence deserves more than your critical cosmetic bullshit. This is not a time to be tugging at your bulges and tearing up. So give all the judgemental head talk a rest.'

Dear Me,

Wahey, look at you – so fresh and so green, grasshopper mumma. You are adulting hard, and I gotta say I'm proud.

I know that right now, you are surrounded by a strange cloudy smog. At night or in the very early morning, a not-so-sweet sensation rises up your neck, a burning or a tightening of gloom that you can usually squash with a flick of the TV remote or a scroll through funny cat videos on YouTube. But not always.

I guess this is what they call doubt. It's quite a foreign feeling to you: the person who was voted most likely to be the next Oprah Winfrey back in Year 10. Confidence is a strange beast, isn't it? Will you ever see the sun again?

Of course you will, you dummy.

Trust me on this one, Suz. This motherhood caper is just the next level to conquer and, at the other end (and, actually, along the way), there are golden experiences and pure joys that are hard to properly describe to someone hasn't felt them. Yet.

Everything that you are doing is perfect. Keep going.

Regret doesn't live here.

Holy heck, what a ride the last few years have been. What a somersault of love and life. You still feel a li'l queasy when you think about it all. You were so single, so free, and partying way too much. You were totally procrastinating and wandering about town, a little lost, but yippee it was fun.

When you met your husband-to-be, it all changed so quickly. Within a wild but brief time you got engaged and married, and your career was looking shipshape. Plans were made to move to New York, or somewhere in Canada, or maybe Morocco, and to live life on the edgier side. It was exciting, crazy, and you finally felt like the gears had clicked in.

Then you fell pregnant.

And woah. Here he is. Here is your son.

There was no time to organise, to think, to prepare or to re-adjust. The months of pregnancy flashed by. You moved cities and found a temporary job, and it seems like he actually arrived almost by accident.

Your bundle of boy.

What a dazzling wonder he is. Even now, four years on, I am still in awe of the human body's – *your* body's – ability to create a tiny human. All those expert little cells that have multiplied and morphed to form a new person, complete with a healthy body, a heartbeat and a soul. It is nothing short of epic. It forces you to believe in something so much greater than what you know. What a force. What a womb.

The first few months will be a tight learning curve of experiences Suz, so I am going to help you cheat on the test. I want to give you seven pieces of advice that are for you and you only. Advice that helped me to get through, things that took me time to learn, and thoughts I wish I'd come to realise earlier. Here goes . . .

Step 1: Suz, take this moment to love your body and appreciate what it has created. I know you want to get back into the gym or to go for a run, but please: chill the feck out. Who gives a shit if it still feels flappy, floppy and somewhat deflated? Remember: that body made that li'l being over there.

The power in your body, its knowledge and its innate intelligence deserves more than your critical cosmetic bullshit. This is not a time to be tugging at your bulges and tearing up. So give all the judgmental head talk a rest. In a few months you will be right back where you were, deadlifting like a boss and fit as a fiddle.

Rest, heal, and throw the stupid scales at the wall.

Step 2: While you are at it with this self-love and preservation, stop it with your stupid social media addiction. Your Instagram feed and Facebook page need to be culled. Unfollow all #fitspo, #shelifts or any form of #fattofittransformation. It is not inspiring you, it's completely undervaluing everything that you are trying to savour right now.

The initial motivation and connection you feel when scrolling through the digital pages is not real. It will come to bite you in your isolated ass. Actually, try not to spend too much time on the internet generally, and DO NOT consult Doctor Google. I mean it, Suz. Stay off mothering forums entirely; they're dangerous places.

Comparing yourself to others will get you nowhere.

Step 3: Get in the habit of being vulnerable and exposed. Let your husband in. You have managed to marry one of the most remarkable beings on the planet, and he loves you. All of you. Tell him the gory and difficult details. He can take it. Tell him how your boobs, back and head hurt; describe the pain of mastitis in all its feverish, achy, blistery hell; and don't hold in your farts for the sake of grace.

Tell him that you need him to be home on time, and working back late is not an option right now. 'Crazy Hour' – your coined phrase, similar to the witching hour – is very, very real and like clockwork. Baby Kaif will scream for about an hour starting at 6.15 p.m. every single night. You will not be able to do anything about it. Actually, you will be able to do one thing. Kaif loves being bounced endlessly on the fitball. Don't bounce on the fitball, Suz.

Step away now and your back will thank you later.

Step 4: Since when has reaching out been so hard? If you were in back in Papua New Guinea and in the village, your home wouldn't have fences; it would hardly have any walls. Family, friends and helpers from all over the island would have come to stay and be by your side, helping. You wouldn't have to ask for help, because that's just the way it is done. You would feel the warmth of your clanswomen. It's hard to build a village of support for yourself in a busy city in Australia, and what you are feeling now is the insurmountable pressure to do it all and to do it alone.

You have this dazed notion that you *should* be able to do it all alone, but you don't have to feel that way. Admit that it's not as easy as you thought and that it's totally bullshit that they left all this hard work out of the baby brochure. Ask for help. Don't let your guilt prevent you from calling your mum, your sister or a bestie. Your friends want to be there for you. They are feeling this change in your life balance too, and want to be included. I know you feel secluded in your own box, but some of this loneliness is self-inflicted. Force yourself to call or send a text.

Be upfront about needing your village.

Step 5: The days when you had your independence and your spontaneity? They really are over. Gone are the days that you can enjoy a good ole-fashioned hangover complete with head in the bowl, followed by burger and beer, only to head out to the dance floor for round two. Let yourself grieve for the old you, for the days past, and then let them go. You know, those past days of yesterday that you never really appreciated.

I agree that it's a pretty big pill to swallow when most of your friends are out in the city and sending you drunken selfies, while you sit up alone to breastfeed at 2 a.m. Engage with the friends you love and completely adore when and how you need to. But remember what I said about comparing? It doesn't help.

Do you, boo-boo, do you.

Step 6: Having said that, if one or two friendships aren't as harmonious or complementary at the moment, allow yourself to let them fade out of view for the time being. Friends come and go and come back again. You don't have the energy or space to harbour guilt about friendship obligations. You can hook back up with them down the track.

Step 7: Being home is easier right now, and that's a fact you need to accept. It's easier to sleep, feed and foster playtime on a four-hourly cycle with all the things you need around you. Going out is scary and challenging and overwhelming and, while you feel isolated and alone sometimes, you also need to take care of you.

You are probably going to roll your eyes and then punch me in the tit for saying this, but why don't you try to enjoy it? Being housebound like this instinctively freaks you out, but there are ways to make it work. Enjoy the simpler (notice I did not say easier) life for once.

. . . So there is my advice, my steps, my tips, my ideas to make these early weeks just that little bit better (again, note that I did not say easier).

Suz, there is a very annoying thing about clichés and that is that they tend to be true. The one that will help you most at this time is not very original, but it sure as hell got me through the toughest of days. Listen up.

The days are long but the years are short.

Doesn't that feel good? As soon as I heard this nugget of wisdom I didn't feel so deserted and alone. Phew, other mothers have also felt that this whole parenting thing this sucks periodically, and probably even daily.

As you keep on keeping on, this little bundle of boy will grow up to reciprocate your love in his own way. Can you believe that your love for him actually continues to grow? The only way is up. He will kiss your nose and hug you tight. He will sing and dance and crack you up on the daily.

This motherhood metamorphosis will bring so many more facets to you, babe; more than you will be able to fathom right now. Right now, you are all boobs and milk and multi-coloured baby shit. You can't see the road ahead, and so all you feel is the loss of the road already travelled. But you will see.

Enjoy the new ride, Suz, with all its new thrills and new spills. I love you.

Suz

Lanai Scarr

*'You need to be a little easier on yourself and remember the scale
of what your body has just undergone. For the past two hundred
and forty days you've had four hearts beating inside you.'*

Holy crap, they're here.

Shit. Wow. Fuuuuckkkkk!!!!!! Is this real? Can you believe it?

You did it. You just gave birth to three babies at once. Triplets:
two identical boys and a girl. Three tiny, part-cooked two-
kilogram humans were pulled out of your belly one by one within
minutes of each other. It was like some sort of weird animal
documentary that suddenly you were a part of.

Lying on the cold operating theatre table, waiting for the
doctor to slice open your towering thirty-four-week triple-packed
belly, you weren't quite sure how things would go.

You'd done birth before – but not like this.

Last time it was eighteen hours in painful posterior labour, on
your birthday, to deliver your daughter Molly. This time it was

an emergency C-section with the enormous pressure of ensuring three babies are all breathing by the end of it.

You were scared – Jim's cord was wrapped around his neck twice, and by the time you made it to the hospital and had seen your doctor you were already ten centimetres dilated.

Once you heard that information, you were keeping your legs tightly closed and willing everything to stop until you could make it to theatre and have all three of your precious miracles delivered safely. A double wrapped cord could have been a death sentence for your now happy, bright, bubbly boy.

When your doctor delivered each baby and held them up over the blue hospital curtain separating you and the crime scene on the other side, all you could think was 'Okay, one more delivered safe and breathing, now for the next one.' The nervous lump in your throat didn't disappear until all three babies were crying and being checked over by their individual team of paediatricians.

There were so many people in the room for the birth, at least thirty. Privacy is not a luxury afforded to one having such an unusual birth. Even the ward receptionist came in to witness the 'spectacle'. But all you were focused on was getting that brief few minutes with those babies, nuzzling close to them before they were whisked off to the special care nursery with your husband, and you off to recovery.

You lie in the recovery room on your own now, with the buzz of machines and hospital staff going back and forth, and it seems quite weird, even dull, after all the excitement of this morning. There is lots of beeping. Nurses and doctors are moving methodically in and out to check on their patients.

James, your husband, is texting you about Edy, who is having trouble breathing on her own and needs to be hooked up to a special machine called a C-PAP, which will help her under-developed lungs to function properly. Before you are out of recovery, Edy will also need surfactant injections direct into her lungs because she's still struggling. And over the course of the night there is talk of flying her up to Sydney if her condition doesn't improve.

Take a deep breath. I'm not telling you this to make you worry, simply to let you know what's coming and that you get through it all. Your children are strong, just like you and your husband, and you will make it through all the ups and downs of this amazing adventure: having four kids under the age of two with a smile on your faces.

Really, you're going to do amazing things by staying strong and doing it your own way. You will have days where it all seems too much, where the house is chaotic and the kids have been cry-ing all day. But you will also have boundless amounts of joy and cuddles and kisses and the love that will beam out of your four children – right into you – will fix the hardest days and weeks, I promise.

You weren't expecting to meet these three new additions to your life today. Your caesarean was planned for tomorrow, your third wedding anniversary. But thankfully those precious bubbas, who are doing so well in the special care nursery right now, had a mind of their own and let you keep at least one date for yourself.

Lanai, your life is going to explode with busy.

For the next thirteen months your boobs will make one litre of breastmilk a day for three babies. Yes, you really will breastfeed triplets for that long. You'll survive on forty-five-minute sleeping blocks when you're on a three-hour feeding rotation at night. You'll somehow stay awake during those night feeds by watching crappy TV on your iPhone in the dark or by playing brain training apps just to keep those eyelids from closing while nursing a baby. Or two.

You'll change close to nine thousand dirty nappies, most of which will require you holding down a screaming child – or three – who thinks being on the change table is akin to torture. It will be like trying to hold onto a fish with vaseline all over your hands while standing in a fragile glass boat. The art of ensuring poo doesn't go everywhere during nappy changes will become your forte, given you will get three lots of practice eight times a day.

Don't forget that your toddler, Molly, will of course want to go to the toilet at the exact moment you're in the middle of changing nappies and will constantly scream at you to come and wipe her bum through the whole daily saga. You toilet-trained her when the babies are six months old because, somehow, you found the time to do that too.

Despite the naysayers, you'll return to work full-time after a year at home. You will successfully juggle a huge family and your passion for writing with near-constant sickness during winter. There are moments when those delightful 'Wonder Weeks' will require that three babies be attached to you at all times. You often spend your entire night's sleep on the floor of one of their bedrooms, patting them.

Once solids arrive it will be pure chaos at feeding time. It will be as if you need to multiply yourself by four in order to get the food delivered quick enough to the three screaming hungry monsters restrained in their high chairs – and Molly too. You'll finish a long day at work and still have to come home to bath and dress four children, who, when they start walking, will find it hilarious to run away from you just as you're setting everything up for their nightly wash.

Even after you get through the craziness of bedtime, you still have to come out and clean up after dinner, pump some breast-milk, and relax with James for a nanosecond before crashing into bed for sleep, wishing you could extend a day to twenty-six hours.

It sounds impossible, but you'll do it, Lanai. You'll do it.

All the emotions you're feeling and things you're thinking about seem a bit too big for the mundane, bland recovery suite you're in. People in here have got their tonsils out and are con-templating the difficult choice of ice cream or custard, while you're trying to get your head around now being a mum of four at the age of twenty-seven.

You're shaking uncontrollably. Your body is in shock and the drugs are beginning to wear off. I know that everything inside you is willing your limbs to stop that damn shaking. You want to see those precious little babies again as soon as you possibly can and you know you can't do that if your body betrays you now.

You need to be a little easier on yourself and remember the scale of what your body has just undergone. For the past two hundred and forty days you've had four hearts beating inside you. At night during the pregnancy, when you lay down to sleep, you could hear the rush of blood in your ears and the pound-ing of those three tiny hearts. Now there's just one heart beating inside of you, exploding with love for the little people in your life. You want to hold them and be near them again. It feels weird lying here in this bed without them.

Take it easy on your body over the next few months and years. You will constantly be at war with your new body shape, and at times run yourself ragged trying to hold down a job, manage a house of seven people (including a live-in au pair) and be slamming yourself to get to the gym at 5.30 a.m. Try and remember during those times that you owe your body – this incredible vessel – a huge debt of gratitude. It has done and will continue to do incredible things.

There will be moments where you feel like you might not cope, but you will get through this. You're a smart, strong, capable woman and one of the world's most organised people, which is lucky because nothing less than a military-style organisation is what you are going to need.

As I write this, all the kids are asleep. It's night-time when the house seems eerily silent. No giggling or squealing or screaming. Despite getting frustrated with how a day might have gone, you often miss them all when they're sleeping and scroll through your phone looking at photos.

Jim, your big boy, is so full of energy and joy. He loves making people happy, his laugh is infectious and he has the cutest little grumpy face. Nate, Jim's identical twin, is snoring away in his bed. He's more reserved than his outgoing big brother. He likes to take his time and really examine things in detail and is not afraid to show his emotions. His happy place is in your arms and he loves one-on-one time with you.

Edy is a mini-you. She is the happiest, most determined person. When she wants something she goes for it with everything she's got. She's cheeky and helping and mothering her siblings, despite being the youngest. Molly is kind and brave and testing, as most toddlers are. But she will handle all the changes that are about to come her way with maturity beyond her years.

The life that lies ahead of you is amazing. Although I know that's hard to believe right now when the present moment is full of fear and uncertainty. You and James will build a foundation of teamwork and you will love and appreciate that man more than you ever thought possible through this amazing journey you're about to embark on. He's doing an incredible job in the special care nursery making key decisions to help them in their first few hours of life. They'll be in humidicribs when you see them, and it will be three weeks before you get to take them home.

James has got this. You've done your job for today. Take a deep breath and try to enjoy being on your own for just a little while longer, as you will rarely get the chance soon. The shaking you're experiencing will stop eventually. I promise. Remember that your body brought life to four children – three all at once – less than an hour ago.

If you only take one thing from this letter, make it this: You are wonder woman, but remember you are also a human woman and make sure you take time to give yourself a break every now and then. Everything doesn't have to be perfect. Your love for your family and children is perfect and that's all that matters.

It is only going to get better from here. Soon, you'll be with those babies again . . .

Lanai x

Karen Pickering

*'This motherhood job is like nothing you could ever imagine.
It's the hardest one you've ever done and all for no pay, with
no training, no management, no OHS guidelines, no leave
for sickness or grief or stress, no weekends, no nights off, and
a triple shift, back to back, on variable sleep.'*

Hey babe,

I know. Like, I really fucking know.

There is nothing I can say that you will comprehend properly in your current sleepless haze. In this moment, you're exhausted and your brain isn't working and you can barely concentrate on *Friday Night Lights* let alone see the structural forces bearing down on you. But I want you to try and understand this one basic truth: It's not you. It's the patriarchy.

You're in love. More powerfully and hopelessly in love than you could ever have predicted. He's probably in your arms right now and you can scarcely breathe for how perfect he is. You are forever caught in between joy and fear and rage and confusion and obsession and just plain old ecstasy. Lots of that is probably how new motherhood has always been, but there is also stuff you are facing that is real and new and of our time and pressing and unfair.

That's what that terror in the pit of your stomach is. Please know that you are normal. This is normal. This is supremely fucked. This is completely unnecessary. Things should not be like this. They are like this, in some sense, for every mother. There is no such thing as normal. You are amazing. I believe you. You matter. You are hurting. It's not your fault.

I wanna try to break down your feelings into individual, separate problems. I'm gonna do this for you, because I know you can barely see straight. First, the way you were treated during the birth will take a long time to deal with and heal from and be okay about. Second, the economy is set up to disadvantage you, especially now that you've had a baby, and your financial stress is legitimate. Third, the fact that you didn't really understand what motherhood would mean is not because you're an idiot or wilfully obtuse or even because you weren't paying attention.

Women conceal the full horror from other women. You couldn't possibly understand until you got here. Even now that you know the reality, it will be very, very difficult to prepare anyone else you know and love before they reach this point. That hurts too.

It's a lot of information to process. So let's go slowly.

Just because Harry's birth resulted in this perfectly divine human being, in relative good health, doesn't mean that what happened to you was okay. There is no easy birth, but yours did not need to be as hard as it was. I know you try to avoid thinking about it, but there is still the phantom subconscious; there are the nightmares. It will be possible to remember some of it more clearly soon. That is good and bad news. Soon it will feel like it happened to someone else, someone that you love and feel sympathy for, but not you. It will help, in a way, to be separate from it, but it will also make you angry.

You'll talk to other women about birth and you'll find out that you aren't the only one who felt bullied by the medical system. You weren't the only one who felt pressured into being induced, who felt dismissed and patronised and infantilised at every turn. You weren't the only one who was shocked at how much talking over you, around you and in spite of you, happened.

You'll come to feel so proud of yourself for pushing back. You really did stick up for yourself, most memorably by sitting up in bed after realising that four doctors were literally standing over you while you were lying down. They were talking about stillbirth and necrotic placentas and hospital policy requiring an induction, and you took a deep breath, listened to your gut, and said no.

You did good that time. You held them off for several days.

I'm afraid it will always feel like you won a few battles but ultimately lost the war.

You'll hit on something soon: that your experience was about structural sexism and misogyny in the medical community, and that you had missed out on opportunities over your whole life to get ready for this. Not only are women ignored, but they're taught to accept it. They're alienated from their bodies. They're conditioned not to trust them. You didn't feel heard or supported or respected at the most vulnerable moment in your life, but this is so much bigger than hospitals, doctors, and the luck of the labour lottery.

Birth is a time when you need to call on all your power. The physical toll alone is unbelievable, and the mental, emotional and psychological impact is hard to measure. You experienced trauma, so you're now having post-traumatic responses. As I have said, that's normal but also fucked.

Your body is pulsing with pain and not all of it is necessarily physical. Are there wounds to your energy? Is the integrity of the body a force field that can be pierced, shattered or broken? Can you repair it? How long does it take to heal conceptual injuries? You haven't even begun to ask these questions, much less answer them. That's okay. There's a lot to unpack and accept and analyse. I'm here and I'm doing the work.

SPEAKING OF WORK, HAVE YOU EVER WORKED THIS GODDAMN HARD IN YOUR MOTHERFUCKING LIFE? This motherhood job is like nothing you could ever imagine. It's the hardest one you've ever done and all for no pay, with no training, no management, no OHS guidelines, no leave for sickness or grief or stress, no weekends, no nights off, and a triple shift, back to back, on variable sleep.

You've also commenced this job – the most important you've ever undertaken – with a colleague who's on his own steep learning curve, where you've never worked on a project of this scale together before, and where the physical workload cannot be shared equally between you.

There's no HR department to work out a pay scale that would reflect the inequity between you and your partner, and, no, your union cannot help this time. Nobody will take your call at the Fair Work Commission. You're a volunteer here and the stakes couldn't be higher. Not to mention that it seems absurd that someone so unqualified could be trusted with this great a responsibility.

I KNOW. WHAT THE FUCK IS GOING ON?

Speaking of work, this full-time job (or three of them) that you now have doesn't leave much time for your own sleeping, or eating or staring lovingly into your baby's eyes while you sing 'Morningtown Ride' by The Seekers. You'll also be going 'back to work' soon. By which I mean the kind of work that our society deems valuable, the kind of work that gets paid.

You'll resent it.

You won't remember why you care about your paid job, even though it's your life's work. You'll hate anything that takes you away from Harry, but you will do it. The upside of this is that you won't be evicted from your crumbling rental property. Oh, and you'll eventually be caffeinated enough to make the connection that your skill set is valuable in making it easier, better and fairer for the women who come next. Your work will limit the future effect of patriarchy on motherhood. Your work helps women and the passion will come back.

You create spaces for women to find each other and fortify themselves, while they work on bigger actions against gender inequality. That's important. You present feminist education in accessible and engaging ways, to people who will take that knowledge and build incredible forms of resistance. Now you have another job: to figure out how to keep doing this while being a good mum and learning to train your feminist lens on motherhood, labour and society.

BUT OF COURSE – WHY DIDN'T YOU JUST SAY SO?

This is where The Village comes in. I've used capitalisation because it's Very Important. Honey, you thought you already knew the importance of community, but you didn't. Not really. You had the structure absolutely right, and your instinct to always look for the woman is bang-on. But now that you're on the other side, you've found a new and unbelievable and bottomless reserve of love for other women: sisters (with babes) in arms.

As so often happens, in this sharing and offering and listening that happens between women, you'll find that you're not alone. You'll find an even deeper, more profound respect and awe and compassion for women, and you'll value your own womanhood more than you ever thought possible. That will be the gift hidden inside this trauma – the solidarity of sisterhood that you've always found solace in will grow into something even more powerful. You'll find your people and you'll keep helping them find each other.

Motherhood will redefine the power of women working together and supporting one another in your own little world, just as it has in the big, bad, real world. It begins with you building an incredible gang of the best, most fundamentally good, people online. Mothers who look after each other by looking out for each other, empathising, hearing, listening, helping, advising, mobilising, and always making you – and each other – feel less alone.

That group might have had an accidental beginning but it's now a deliberately purposeful project. Look what you are discovering there. You didn't have a mother – not that you never experienced mothering, you did, and it was beautiful but sporadic – but to *be* a mother now, and to do it in concert with other mothers, feels like the greatest honour imaginable. Now you really understand what a mother is. What she means.

You are still the same person. Yes, still. Inside you beats the same heart and the brain ticks faster than ever and remembers everything. Guts that got you this far, got you through everything, kept you alive and even brought others courage and strength – this is at the core of your being. After all you've seen and felt and experienced, it's your guts that makes you different (to others) but the same (as ever).

It's confusing. Don't worry, my love, because I promise it's all going to be okay. Look around you. It's a glorious summer's day in the city you love and while you don't venture outside enough, there are reasons for that too. Go gently with your heart and give yourself time and space to heal.

Look how disciplined and determined and self-aware you showed yourself to be today: ready to rejoin the world as a new person, with a new person, and, no matter what anyone implies or flat out says, that's a big fucking deal. In that early period of Harry's life you found it in yourself to be brave and to leave the protection of home, venture out and attend a policy launch with a newborn: participating in your community of women, celebrating the fact that they are stronger together.

You did this today because you wanted to tell Harry that he was there, at the beginning of something momentous. Change is possible, and he will grow up knowing all the women who fought for him too. One day you'll be able to tell him that he was passed around with love between Mary and Tanja and Maria. One day he can read about their giant contributions in books and articles, and he can feel proud and special knowing they were pleased to see his sweet face in a space made glorious by women.

You want Harry to know that he was joyfully welcomed at a government event with acceptance and warmth. That wouldn't have been possible a generation before, when mothers and babies didn't belong at work, in public or at celebrations of civic importance. Things are changing and his world will be different and better than the one that came before because it will properly value the work and contribution of women. You have to keep believing that . . .

Now here's the big one, babe. It's not in your head. You're not imagining it. Things seem really unfair right now, like the world is conspiring against you. It feels like you shouldn't have to be battling alone and like you shouldn't be made to carry such an enormous burden. It feels like the deck is stacked against you, stacked against mothers, stacked against all women. That's because it is. Things really are unfair.

It's set up this way to benefit other people, people who aren't you and who aren't women. This is what I mean by patriarchy being at the centre of your complex web of feelings. It's not your fault that you're struggling, because the system is designed to make you feel as though all of the difficulties you're having are the result of your personal failings.

I want to be clear: you are not to blame for how hard this is, nor are you deficient because you're hurting right now. From your birth, to Harry's, and as far ahead as you can see, women are damned if they do and damned if they don't. Induce or don't induce, vaginal or caesarean, breastfeed or formula, co-sleep or sleep train, go to work or don't go to work, baby-led-weaning or baby-fed-by-spoon-ing, carrier or pram, day care or nanny, public or Steiner, dummy or thumb, forward-face or rear-face – it actually makes no difference what a mum chooses, she will be judged for it with a ferocity and spite that dads simply do not face. You might have sensed this was true before, but now it's written on your body, pulsing in your temples and running through your veins.

I know it doesn't feel like it, but you're actually doing so great. Eventually you'll get some sleep, Harry will get even more gorgeous, and one day you'll see the weird and surprising truth that all the mothers you love, all the women you look up to and see as fierce warriors wrapped in warm softness, full of wisdom and patience and the truest love, the ones who look after everyone and keep us all alive – you're totally one of them.

All my love, dear girl.

KP x

Nareen Young

'When my baby girl comes along, I look forward to getting to know her in the same way I did her brother. That slow, fascinating emergence of personality and traits that are somehow surprising but, at the same time, not.'

Dear Nareen,

Here you are holding your great big girl. She has this intense green-eyed gaze that is somehow accusatory. Your arms wrap around her as she sleeps, your fingers playing with her auburn hair and touching her translucent skin.

Translucent skin? What?

Nobody tells you that genetics are a funny thing and that you could be welcoming a snowflake-skinned baby into your midst, surrounded as you always have been with the many varieties – from golden syrup to leather – that the Australian mix can produce.

'We've never had one like that before,' said your mother upon first sighting. It never even occurred to you that your daughter wouldn't have skin just like your own, just like her golden-skinned brother does. This newborn girl is a woman of her dad's family, translucent like all of them, with those old, hardy picture post-card genes from Ennis and Kinvara popping out at King George V in Newtown. This country never ceases to amaze me.

Why didn't anyone tell you that you could produce a baby like this one? Already having had one child, you thought that you knew all there was to know about popping them out.

This new girl is so huge, even bigger than her brother was, and so alert. In her hospital photo she smiles knowingly, like there's some excellent secret only she knows. She's so interac-tive that the head obstetrician, already familiar with her as the large subject of a 'high-risk' pregnancy, comes around with a gaggle of medical students for a look, saying to his pupils: 'I just had to show her to everyone! They didn't believe that we have one who's like a three-month-old baby already.' Look, they did, and they got her to interact too. Nobody told you that you might give birth to an exhibition piece.

Nobody told you that this birth, so carefully managed because of the pre-eclampsia that popped up unexpectedly and ferociously last time around, would result in this great big piece of a girl. A girl who would work herself into such a grumpy tizzy at the temerity of being removed from her comfy thirty-nine-week spot under your rib, that she gave herself apnoea. Twice.

We really didn't need that trip to ICU immediately post-birth, girlfriend, we really didn't. But, you see, our gorgeous girl had cried herself into losing her breath. I recall sitting there and chatting after the birth. I held our girl and heard my dad's calm, modulated voice saying, 'Reen, is the baby a bit blue?' I've known that professional lifeguard voice all my life. I recognised that

I needed to panic at the sound of its calm, emphatic modulation. That was a brief but very real emergency.

Nobody tells you that pregnancy might be different the second time around. There was so much more sick, all the time (sitting on the toilet vomiting into the bath being my personal morning highlight). There were different cravings (tomatoes, never enough fresh pineapple juice and almonds, almonds and more almonds). And different movements – my girls aren't jumpy like my sons were. Instead they're slow, languid and strong. And different aches and pains – she stands on my kidneys, I'm sure.

The pre-eclampsia that happened last time you were pregnant has created an anxiety so intense that you thought your head would explode. There were many years spent thinking about and planning this pregnancy, worrying endlessly about its return.

Nobody told you that its effects wouldn't be felt until three days after the birth. This time the evil magic happened later. Up and up and up it went, your blood pressure sky-rocketing on the dreaded day three.

Pre-eclampsia is a bitch that you convince yourself is your own fault. It's the fault of the incompatibility of your ancient, unknown, mysterious bloodlines – a bloodline that presents what this country disapprovingly terms 'health issues' – combined with those of Mr West Clare. It's so strange that a couple with such profound compatibility should have this physical incompatibility that leads to such wild unpredictability in pregnancy and birth.

Why doesn't anyone tell you about pre-eclampsia? Why doesn't anyone tell you that you might get it? And that it's a wild, unpredictable ride that can take you to the precipice of death and back again? Why didn't anyone tell you back in your first pregnancy that those concerned looks between the midwives aren't just warranted but spell a terrifying conclusion?

If you realised the severity, perhaps you would have taken it more seriously. For God's sake, in that first pregnancy you were going to work, trying to prove that you could do everything, administering delegate meetings and writing bulletins and running a union election campaign. *STOP IT*, I want to yell back at you in the past. *It's time to go home. You can lose this baby if you push too hard. You can die. And so might he.*

Your first baby, a boy, was born after you had to be induced at thirty-nine weeks. Your blood pressure was so high they thought things might go astray. It was a precaution. The next thing you knew, you're being run – literally run – to the theatre and then there's an emergency caesar with seven doctors present, because your blood pressure is that high and they can't find his heartbeat. It was like ER, without Clooners.

Why didn't anybody warn you that the doctors would tell your beautiful, passionate, soft, loving hazel-eyed man that you and the baby might not be okay? Why didn't anybody tell you that you'd wake up in recovery asking 'Where's my baby?' That the sound of the lovely nurse saying 'Oh Nareen', with all the drama of the last few hours in her voice, is something you'll never, ever forget.

After all the shock, you finally get that baby in your arms, with his long legs and his gorgeous red butt, and you know why nobody tells you. Nobody tells you because it doesn't matter. Nobody tells you because once that baby is in your arms all the fear and panic and drama are gone. All gone.

That big, gorgeous blonde boy with his head covered in down. Rubbing my lips along his beautiful caesarean-shaped head.

His calm little self held tight against my chest, making his presence known. Everybody *does* tell you about that part, but you don't believe it till you experience it for yourself: the overwhelming sense of intensity, of love, of calm and of purpose.

When my baby girl comes along, I look forward to getting to know her in the same way I did her brother. That slow, fascinating emergence of personality and traits that are somehow surprising but, at the same time, not. This long getting-to-know-you period of trying each other on for size. All this with an unknown goal and destination. For me, babyhood and childhood really is just a long period of getting to know each other.

And here she is. My girl.

For her, I feel the same intense love I did for my son but in a different way. I'm holding her and that weird, overwhelming intensity of love is back. I'm holding her fingers that are so like mine, kissing her full little lips, stroking her perfect eyebrows and gazing at her long eyelashes. I really do make babies with excellent eyelashes. I'm thinking about how cool it will be to have this beautiful auburn hair to play with as she grows up and suddenly I'm worried for her in a way I never was about her brother.

Nobody tells you about how you'll be so desperate to protect her from all the things. Can I create a world for her where she won't find out about all the pressures of girlhood and doesn't have to worry about them? How can I make it so she's never violated, never has sexist assumptions made about her? How can I make it so she can wear what she wants, throw balls if she wants, surf if she wants, marry another girl if she wants, and at the same not have to do any of those things if that's what she wants?

And the truth is that I can't give her that protection. I can't hide her away from this world. I can't, on my own or in the many collectives of women I work among. All I can do is love her and make sure she knows that she will always have her dad's and my profound, deep love. I can make sure she knows how very lucky we are to have her.

That our love for her is driven by the values we share and the things we both hold dear. I want her to know that she is loved, and life is pretty good for us women, despite the girl things and the identity things she will inevitably run into in this country of ours.

She doesn't look like me. Nobody told me that could happen.

Love,
Nareen

Gorgi Coghlan

*'That gorgeous girl may very well be the only child you can have.
In the near future, you're going to face some challenging chapters
with your fertility. It will be a confronting journey. There will be
tears and lots of them. There will be feelings of deep inadequacy.'*

Dear GC,

How are you holding up, sister?

You're a little shocked, I know. First, there was the emergency
caesarean that came four and half weeks early. Next, the cord
was wrapped around her little neck. Then came the infection.
It was all pretty full-on, hey?

You can take a breath now.

There was never going to be a peaceful, relaxed entrance into
the world for this little soul. She was always going make a grand
arrival. She's fabulously impatient, spirited and magnificent.
Everything you'd ever want in a daughter. Your love for her is a
love like none you've ever known. So full, so rich and protective.

Although you were planning on a drug-free natural birth (let's be fair now, who were you kidding, GC?), that isn't how it went. Coming as early as it did, the birth of your daughter was complicated, scary and traumatic.

What you mistook for Braxton Hicks was, in fact, four long days of pre-labour. Do you remember watching that Geoffrey Rush film *The King's Speech* and grasping for breath every twenty-five minutes or so? They. Were. Contractions.

A night in hospital caused your waters to break, which was a good result according to the midwives. Then the real fun began. The full-blown contractions kicked in and although it was pain like you have NEVER EVER experienced, you were almost relieved that things actually seemed to be progressing.

Your midwife was exceptional and, thankfully, very experienced. She noticed your baby's heart rate plummeting with each contraction and knew something was wrong. In the moments that followed, things moved fast, but to you it was as if everything was playing in slow motion.

The obstetrician was there, telling you that the baby had to come out NOW. There were injections to stop the contractions and stop the labour progressing further. The bed was whisked along the corridor and your husband was being fitted with scrubs like he was in an episode of *Grey's Anatomy*.

Despite the chaos and anxiety, you were calm. You closed your eyes, went into your deepest consciousness and repeated the mantra: My baby is safe. My baby is safe. My baby is safe. And she was.

A mere twenty minutes later, you were holding her on your chest for the first time. Her tiny fingers were grasping at yours. Her eyes were unable to focus on this new place. You and your devoted husband experienced the unparalleled feeling of being a parent: a feeling that hasn't gone away since. You were overcome with overwhelming love, relief, gratitude and connection to this little person.

I'm proud to say that you've always managed to maintain that gratitude, GC. It makes my heart full to know how you keep looking at her with wonder, checking on her religiously throughout the night. Crying happy tears when you hold her. You know how lucky you are and how precious this life is.

What you don't know yet, in those early weeks, is just *how* precious.

That gorgeous girl may very well be the only child you can have. In the near future, you're going to face some challenging chapters with your fertility. It will be a confronting journey. There will be tears and lots of them. There will be feelings of deep inadequacy.

You will fret and become extremely anxious about only having one child. You'll imagine catastrophic situations where she will be taken away from you. Your fear will tempt you to pull her in closer and closer and never let her go.

You try IVF. You try everything you can to control a situation that is completely out of your control. You need to do this to eventually reach a place of peace. By accepting that you can only control this moment, right now, you'll learn to be present in it. Your daughter seems to somehow understand this, even when she is still tiny, and helps navigate you down the path from fear to peace.

Eventually you will process the pain and surrender your heart to accepting things as they are and gratitude replaces guilt. Ironically, it makes you become an even better mother: a mother who relishes every second with her little girl, a mother who is just so grateful to be a mum in the first place.

When your daughter comes home from school and asks if she can have a brother or a sister, it doesn't cause you pain any longer. You're able to hug her, smile and remind her that you're trying your best.

This painful journey opens your heart, heals your hurt and makes you grateful for the joy that is your healthy and happy party of three. Of course, there will be deep sadness, but along with this sadness comes the wonderful realisation that your daughter is more than enough. In fact, she is extraordinary.

You've had a pretty good life, GC, but right now you have no idea of the joy that lies ahead with this little girl. She is truly a wise soul who leads you and your husband through magical chapters.

She likes horses and you'll ride together, but she won't love them like you do, and you'll laugh at that. She has the most angelic voice and she fills the house with song every day. You often catch yourself listening in wonder and thanking the universe you have been lucky enough to have a daughter for whom music is life.

She will challenge you, reflect both your good and bad parenting techniques and be a really crappy eater most of the time. Her wit and sense of humour will continue to amuse and frustrate you. She's a cracker.

As you sit and hold her, in these embryonic first weeks of motherhood, I hear you promise her that she will have the perfect life. Oh, GC, always the perfectionist, aren't you? Yes, you will give her an awesome, loved, supported, hilarious life, a dynamic and extremely privileged life. But it won't be perfect. And that's okay.

You're human. You're impatient, over-protective at times, terrible without sleep and prone to anxiety. Sometimes you focus so much on getting everything 'right' that there's no room left for fun, for play. I want you to keep meditating and staying in the moment. Practice gratitude and open your heart. You'll reap the reward a thousand times over. Trust me on this one.

You're a great mum, GC. Loving, affectionate, playful and extremely intuitive. So take it easy, sister. You're ace. Go with the flow and try to be kind to yourself. Trust this crazy universe and keep opening that big heart to what your spirited and unique little daughter will teach you. So let it go, GC. Laugh. Play. Surrender.

Lots of love from your older – and hopefully wiser – self.

GC xx

Katie 'Monty' Dimond

'Instead of heading to the doctors, you decide to
"see how you are in the morning". This is
stupid, Monty. This is very stupid.'

Dear New Mamma Monts,

Congrats on the babe and all that. How wild is it gazing at that mini man you totally made? So tiny, so delicious, so many bodily functions that exit from such minute little holes.

This is just a quick letter to let you know that now is the perfect time to strap in. You are about to embark on an extremely wild love ride. There will be times when you are going to feel like you might combust from the all-consuming, intoxicating, indescribable love that will swallow you whole.

Then, of course, there will be times when you will pine for your old extremely self-indulgent life, where you had the freedom to do simple things like urinate without the backing track of a squealing child. Oh, the joys of it all.

Anyway, I digress. The main reason I write today is to chat to you about those two mounds that protrude from your chest. This is a little letter of warning, I guess you could say . . . A little letter of warning about your boobs.

Before falling pregnant they struggled to fill an A cup, didn't they? They were kinda pathetic to be honest. Then, while growing a human inside of you, they blossomed into a decent handful – hooray! Then, three days after your son exited your body, you legit got some very, very impressive norgs.

Monts, you will indeed fall wildly in love with your new assets and although they look truly fabulous and your cleavage game is real strong, they will soon require more attention than the tiny alien-like human you are now responsible for.

The books tell you all about the baby. Nobody warns you about the boobs. A little inflammation called mastitis is literally going to hit you in the tit, not once, not twice, but five times over the next few months. Childbirth will almost feel like it tickled compared with the agony this moll will bring you.

Sorry, babe, but this is a letter to inform you, warn you, prepare you and provide some super-valuable advice about the pain that is to come. Obviously, it's too late to help you – bummer about that – but maybe some other broad who is reading over your shoulder will be spared.

Your first encounter will come out of the blue when you are at a swimming meet watching Michael Klim race. That in itself is extremely odd because you have no interest in swimming and haven't been to a pool since your lessons in grade six.

You will jump out of your skin when mates invite you to check out old Klimbo pound the pool. After a week of solitude, you'll feel so isolated by the baby that anything outside the walls of your home sounds enticing. You've basically been velcroed to the couch.

While watching the people swim the laps, you feel flu-like symptoms coming over you. Your first mistake will be shaking it off as nothing. Instead of bolting to the doctor to get your mitts on antibiotics PRONTO, you will proceed to soak up the freedom of the indoor pool environment and relish the achievement of leaving the house.

After the exhilaration of watching people you don't know race in water, you then go out to dinner with your mates and the seven-day-old. Oh babe . . . Bless you and your laughably ambitious new mum endeavours. By the time dessert arrives, you will be aching all over like you have the plague and your tits will literally feel like they are on fire. It isn't the fun burning feeling either. It seriously bloody hurts.

Instead of heading to the doctors, you decide to 'see how you are in the morning'. This is stupid, Monty. This is very stupid. The night that follows will see you wince, moan and cry when you whack your mini man on for a feed (which is pretty much every two hours).

You will drench your bed with sweat while you shake like a polaroid picture in your milk-soaked pyjamas and cry at the mere thought of your baby coming within a metre of your nips.

Your baby daddy will ring the new parents' helpline as he is pretty convinced from the sounds exiting your body that you are about to die. He will follow instructions and promptly run you a boiling hot bath and order you to get in it and start milking your own breasts.

As you lay in the scalding water, rubbing the lumps in your veiny boobs, chunks of milk will literally float out. CHUNKS! As sick as you are, your mind will be blown away by the actual milky chunks bobbing around the bath. It's both magical and kind of gross at the same time.

That is your first dance with the devil that is mastitis. You will endure it another four times because you are a martyr who refuses to give up breastfeeding your child. (Something I'm really proud of you for.)

Over the weeks that follow, you will consume more anti-biotics than all the cows in the world (fact) and rub around 643 milk chunks out of your boobs (never not fascinating). You will audibly squeal as your baby latches on, wipe blood from your nipples on several occasions and make the local fruit grocer think you have a weird obsession with cabbages.

Mastitis is a nasty old bitch and she creeps into the blissful baby bubble without a minute's warning. So on that note I will sign off with some tips as a seasoned mastitis mother. Here are some musts and must nots for the next little while:

1. DO clean your mitts before popping your child on your teet. Always. If you are a nose picker (and let's be honest, many of us are) there is a strong correlation between nose bacteria and mastitis. Basically, don't pick your nose then breastfeed your baby. That's a good mummy.

2. DO NOT get heavy-handed with your breast pump too early on. I pumped like a demon thinking it would be cute for my baby daddy to give some bottles to our offspring. I ended up producing more and

more milk, because my body got the instruction that I needed to feed a tiny nation of children. My baby didn't want all that milk and then . . . You know the drill.

3. DO get to the doctor the second you feel a niggle of any flu-like symptom or have particularly sore boobs. If they prescribe antibiotics, pop that pill immediately and finish the whole course.

4. DO keep your fridge well stocked with cold cabbage leaves. They ease the pain and cool the teat when put in a bra.

5. DO run a bath as hot as you can handle and submerge your whole body including your bazookas, while you wait for the antibiotics to kick in. Have a good feel for the lumps and lightly massage those pricks out. Enjoy the spectacle of floating milk muck. Seriously.

6. DO NOT be hard on yourself, you mean old bitch. You are letting nobody down if breastfeeding becomes too hard and too painful for you. Formula is grouse.

7. DO NOT take these tips on board with a grain of salt. They aren't floaty, hippy, silly 'maybe I will' advice. They're the real thing. Inhale them and take them as gospel.

You are entering what feels like a whole new world. And truthfully it is.

You now have a living, breathing miniature human to nurture and love and mould into a future grown-up. Pressure level is at its maximum. But please know that you have got this.

You and your baby will grow and learn together and even though some days will be shitful, loads of others will be utterly blissful.

Love to you and my boobs.

Monty

Laura Chalmers

'You know that while raising Leo has its challenges, loving him feels like the easiest job in the world. You wonder why it took you so long to get here and why you denied yourself this lovely little man and the pure joy of being his mum.'

Dear Laura,

In one respect your pregnancy was like everyone else's: all about the numbers.

Forty weeks (plus two). 3.22 kilograms. Single birth. First child.

But in your case it was about one number in particular. Six minutes.

If Leo had been born six minutes later, at noon instead of 11.54 a.m., you wouldn't have had to sheepishly ask your doctor if you could stay one extra night in hospital. Under hospital rules, that fourth night would have been automatic.

Six weeks later and those six minutes seem immaterial. At the time? Crucial.

As the midwives were readying your departure forms and everything seemed fine, you knew that you needed that one extra night of reassurance. You needed someone to tell you that your body wasn't going to crumble beneath you and that your child was going to continue breathing beyond the security of the hospital suite.

At any other time in your life, you would have relished the chance to get home. But this was not any other time. Before Leo was born you convinced yourself that you would need only twenty-four hours in hospital and then you'd be impatient to have your newborn home and to yourself. In reality, due to the stalled admission of an epidural in the final stages of childbirth, your numb legs were unable to hold you up on the day he was born, let alone walk you and your son out of hospital. This was just one example, of many, where your expectations of motherhood would fall well short of reality.

On the day Leo was born you woke early, knowing from the increasingly frequent contractions what would lie ahead. You took a photo of the sunrise to document the day for your soon-to-be-born son and chirpily texted your obstetrician: *Seems today is the day!*

Little did you know that despite drinking raspberry leaf tea for weeks, undergoing pre-childbirth acupuncture and attending 'labour-ready' prenatal yoga sessions, labour was going to hit you with a ferocity that couldn't have been foreseen. From cold shivers to hot flushes to the primal screams that you heard coming from other women during antenatal classes. In the last few hours you didn't open your eyes once, so difficult was the pain to confront.

Childbirth was not the only thing you headed into blind to its true intensity.

Next came life with a newborn.

Sure, you knew things would be different when you had this baby. You knew that little flicker of a heartbeat on the ultrasound screen would mean less sleep, years of trying to juggle some sort of work/life balance, fewer overseas trips to New York on a whim. You knew it would change your relationship with your husband and fundamentally alter your roles from that of 'husband' and 'wife' to the role you previously associated only with your parents, that of 'mum' and 'dad'.

But what no baby book you read, antenatal class you endured or conversation you had with a new mum prepared you for was the depth of the emotional connection you would feel with this baby once he was placed in your arms. Becoming a mum will fundamentally rewire you, Laura, in ways nobody properly prepared you for.

Eleven fifty-four a.m. will be the dividing line between two very clear stages in your life: pre-Leo and post-Leo.

Post-Leo, your own identity feels obscured by the ray of light that is your son. Your heart is beating outside of your body now and all of your cares and fears and anxieties seem to have been transferred into his tiny little frame. His needs have entirely taken priority over your own. You have foregone sleep, sanity, sustenance, spicy food, shots of caffeine and glasses of wine, because your baby boss has greedily demanded it of you. You battle with knowing where you end and he begins.

The first time Leo is apart from you, one hour after his birth, you are shocked by how unsettled it makes you feel. The midwife takes Leo from your chest, places him in a bassinet and wheels him out of the room to the maternity suite. He is in a different room to you: separated for the first time in his newfound life.

It feels like the first of many small steps of independence that Leo will take away from you. You made him, yet he will one day make his own way through the world.

You used to spend a lot of time thinking about the 'perfect' time to have a child. Now you only wonder how you possibly lived thirty-two years of your life without Leo. Without his little hand in yours, his morning cuddles, his unique ability at only 51 cm long to somehow monopolise all the corners of your queen bed. Your reasons for delaying motherhood seem utterly superficial now that he is here, looking at you with his wrinkly face and summoning you with his squeaky excuse for a cry.

In 2015, there were 305 377 babies born in Australia.

Leo was but one of them.

You had expected that motherhood – one of the most natural things in the world, experienced by so many – would be simply another stage in your frenetic life. Your social media feeds were filled with friends who appeared to have effortlessly given birth and loved their life as new mums. Instead, you have been overwhelmed at times by just how challenging it can be to look after one little human who is completely dependent on you for everything they need to survive. Milk, warmth, affection, tepid baths and soothing cuddles. Beyond his immediate needs, you know you are going to need to be his person, his role model, the one who explains the things he doesn't understand, who teaches him basic values and the ways of the world.

No one talked to you before Leo's birth about the anxiety that would come with caring for a small, defenceless human. You already love this baby so much that you worry yourself sick about keeping him safe and well. You feel his feet to make sure they're not in need of socks and you take his temperature (more times than you will ever admit) when he's burning up. You wonder how you will cope if anything bad ever happens to this child. How will you shield him from cruel people and broken hearts, sickness and bad news?

When your husband returns to work you will find yourself overwhelmed at times by the job of keeping this tiny little human nourished and nurtured. You have advised a Prime Minister, you have travelled to war zones, and functioned on minimal sleep in the most difficult of work environments. Yet satisfying this child has, on some days, felt like an equally formidable task. You feel an even greater respect for single parents who don't have the much-needed respite afforded by a partner returning at the end of a work day.

Friends warned you that having a baby would change your relationship with your husband forever. That the focus would shift from each other to being irretrievably all about your child.

You view this differently. The love in your little family is shared between the three of you now, but it is no less intense or deeply felt. The joy your husband gets from parenting overwhelms you. You thought you couldn't possibly love him any more until you saw him with your son. The pride he takes in your son's incremental achievements, the adoration he shows in his gentle gestures of touch, the way he quietly hums to Leo as he falls asleep or reads to him even though he is clearly too small to understand the book. You treasure the special time that they spend together in the morning, when your son contentedly sleeps off his milk coma on his dad's chest, his little body rising and falling with every breath.

You have both found yourself moved to tears by little gestures from a baby too young to understand their complexity. There is the grasping of a finger, a muddled messy kiss on a cheek, an arm around the shoulder that feels like a fumbled attempt at a hug. You look forward to a time where there is no ambiguity about the intent of these actions.

That is not to say that having a child doesn't pose challenges for any relationship, regardless of how strongly it is forged. You are both despairingly sleep-deprived, you are parenting novices and you're petrified of somehow hurting this little thing that sleeps beside your bed.

Baby technology will confound you with its complexity, proving to be more time-intensive than furniture flat packs. You and your husband will spend an inordinate amount of time trying to work out how to adjust the straps on Leo's baby capsule on the day you take him home. And the first attempt at setting up the supposedly-simple-to-assemble pram – on a hot, humid afternoon – will almost bring the two of you to tears. The baby will accidentally fall off the change table, and the bed. And you'll do your best not to blame each other when that happens.

There are many things about parenting you'll have to learn the hard way. The rare day you don't put a spare nappy and a spare outfit in the car will be the day that both are, quite urgently, required. Unfortunately for you, you will discover this during a catch-up with your employer in which you will be attempting – rather unsuccessfully – to show that you are nailing this parenting business.

That pre-baby decision to purchase a designer cream couch will also be shown to be an incredibly poor one. By the time Leo is six weeks there isn't a bodily substance of his that isn't firmly embedded into its cushions.

You'll also learn to be kind to your body, which has just performed the ultimate physical triumph. It still feels bruised and sore and squishy, but also somehow elastic in its ability to morph back into some form of your pre-baby self. It has taken time for those phantom kicks in your tummy to stop and for you to allow yourself the utter delight of reading a book while lying on your stomach again.

You still reflexively place your hand on your tummy when you're talking about Leo, despite the fact that he lies beside you, his own little independent person now. Breastfeeding is becoming easier, but that doesn't mean that it won't hurt or force you onto antibiotics or leave you ravenously hungry at all hours. Some days you will feel like this child is taking absolutely everything you have to give.

You will experience a newfound closeness with and an appreciation of your mother and the experiences she went through raising you and your siblings. The reality of the baby she lost when you were just a little girl will finally hit you with full force. You will feel a gut-wrenching sense of horror at how heartbreaking it must have been to deliver a baby that breathed and lived but was not strong enough to make it home from hospital. At the time, you only vaguely understood the notion of losing a brother, but now you fully understand the concept of losing a son.

When people told you about how life would change as a parent, the advice focused on what you would lose. Sleep-ins, skin free of stretch marks, spontaneous dinner plans and full-time salaries. You know now what a baby can take from you, emotionally and physically. There are days as a parent that have not been happy, or easy, to endure. But you know that all of this is surpassed, for you, by what you have gained – this inquisitive sweet-smelling bundle of a baby who makes your life feel fuller, and richer, than it has ever been. You know that while raising Leo has its challenges, loving him feels like the easiest job in the world.

You wonder why it took you so long to get here and why you denied yourself this lovely little man and the pure joy of being his mum.

Love,
Laura

Georgina Dent

'Don't even think about denying yourself one of those glorious bagels with your coffee. If there is ever a time for creature comforts in the form of complex carbohydrates laden with cream cheese and berry jam, it is now.'

Dear Georgie,

Right now there is so much you have no way of knowing. You have stepped into a new world where nothing is familiar. You don't recognise the skin or the body you are in. You don't recognise the life you are leading. It feels like a mix-up. Somehow, *you* have become a mother.

You are, quite literally, shattered. Your body is still recovering from a childbirth that was not empowering but excruciating. Although it culminated in something truly wonderful – your darling daughter Issy – the journey there was long and arduous.

You know those people who end up delivering their baby on the side of the road because it happened so quickly? Try to be like them next time. You could have driven from your little flat in Oxford to London and flown from Heathrow to Sydney and then back to Hong Kong, and you *still* wouldn't have had a baby in transit.

Your labour was extended and traumatic, and it's okay to say that. It's okay that you feel fragile. After what you went through, there is no way you could feel any other way. From the future, I'm happy to assure you that you will never have another labour like it. And, despite what you are thinking in this moment, you *will* choose to go through labour again. Twice.

In those early weeks you will be pining for the day, or even the hour, where you will wake up of your own accord. Summonsed to consciousness by something other than the cry of a bundle who needs your body, or mammaries so engorged they need the baby. NOW.

Currently, your body is providing all the nourishment Issy needs and it is a round-the-clock proposition that makes working in the law firm seem idle. Forget a weekend or even a single day off – you barely get an hour off. The feeds come around so quickly and they take such a long time. Being needed so much – and so often – is daunting.

You will wonder if you can do it. You can. You will wonder if you will suffocate under the weight of responsibility. You won't. You will wonder if the fact you are even wondering these things makes you a bad mum. It doesn't.

As you are learning, the first few weeks as a parent are highly charged with a ferocious kind of love and awe that is unlike anything you've ever felt. You *love* the tiny bundle who you still can't fathom that your body grew. But your love is laced with fear. She is precious and perfect and she is yours, which is still, understandably, a point of some confusion.

Who would *ever* have predicted that you, who underwent five operations for endometriosis, battled with Crohn's disease and spent years on nasty immunosuppressants from the age of nineteen, would fall pregnant and grow a baby so easily? Not the specialist obstetrician your GP suggested you consult, and certainly not you or Nick.

Ten months ago, three days into your married life, when you boarded that flight from Sydney to London you knew your life was about to change. You thought the extent of that change would be setting up a new life in a quaint university town for the next two years. You didn't expect to welcome a child before your first wedding anniversary, but, by a stroke of luck you will never fail to be grateful for, the unexpected happened.

However, all of the gratitude and love in the world won't help you now, not practically anyway. Neither gratitude nor love will get up in the night and feed your baby. Neither gratitude nor love can manifest a short break in play during 'witching hour' so you can eat your dinner while it's hot. Neither gratitude nor love can produce a short and succinct manual with handy instructions on exactly what Issy needs and when.

That manual? It doesn't exist and it never will.

Instead, you will have to rely on your own intuition. You will ask everyone you know – and even people you don't – for advice. You will consult and curse an array of baby books and you will fumble through. In time, you will very genuinely miss being able to spend so much of a single day simply feeding Issy. You will miss the long feeds. That is unimaginable right now but, then again, so is almost everything.

It's hard to imagine how you will reconcile the all-consuming task of nurturing your baby with anything else. It's hard to imagine how you will ever exist as something other than a walking milk bar.

But in just a few short weeks you will occasionally wake up without your feeding singlet being drenched in milk and your breasts ready to explode. You will shower without milk gushing everywhere. And at some point – albeit a little way down the track – you won't even need to wear feeding singlets. (Note to Past Georgie: Those ugly, flimsy feeding bras will stay unused in your underwear drawer for years to come. Throw them out now. The singlets are your friend.)

There will come a day where you won't spend every evening from now until eternity rocking and swaddling and feeding in a bid to coax Issy into her night-time slumber. You will not spend the hours leading into the evening anxiously wondering how and when the night's 'witching hours' will unfold.

A bedtime will present itself sooner than you think and the evenings will be yours again. You will develop an intense and abiding appreciation of the hours between 7 p.m. and whenever you choose to hop into bed. You will cherish this child-free time forever more. You will never take it for granted again.

You will get really good at eating one-handed, but it's a skill you won't need forever. Sadly, you will never master the art of spreading butter and vegemite on toast with one hand. It is beyond your dexterity, so rather than persevering? Accept it. Put Issy in the bouncer for the thirty-five seconds it will take to get your toast appropriately prepped.

You will eat dinner sitting down again. You will even enjoy the use of both hands, and, occasionally, this will correspond with your husband also sitting down for dinner with both of his hands free.

Hearing your baby cry won't get easier. It never will. But you will get better at recognising what the cry means and there will be less crying altogether.

Your body – inside and out – will recover. You will move freely and comfortably again. Your gigantic breasts will eventually deflate. Your tummy will never be toned again, but, honestly, it never was! It will, however, feel like yours once more.

Don't even think about denying yourself one of those glorious bagels with your coffee. If there is ever a time for creature comforts in the form of complex carbohydrates laden with cream cheese and berry jam, it is now. There will be time to rectify that later.

At this point in time, survival is your only priority.

Drink coffee. Splurge on chocolate. Let the house be messy. Talk to your friends. Binge on episodes of *The West Wing*. Sit with the women in your mother's group often. They will be your salvation on many, many occasions for the next twelve months. Enjoy a few glasses of wine. Sleep whenever you can. Not forever and ever, *obviously*, but for the next little while, because this bit right now? It's the hardest. Almost inexplicably, having a second and third baby will feel like nothing compared to what you are facing now.

I know that will shock you, because after the labour you had you are still completely flummoxed that any woman anywhere has ever subjected herself to childbirth more than once. But many do and you will be one of them.

Georgie, there is so much you have no way of knowing right now.

The good news is that most of it is better than you could ever imagine.

Love,
Georgie

Kara Keys

*'Any alternative was better than the nightmare you were living.
I hated myself and I hated my child. I hated my partner, my
life, and it felt as if this horror show, which I enthusiastically
signed up for, would go on forever.'*

Dear Kara,

It's taken a while for me to get this letter sorted in my head. The
idea of writing to my past self, as a reflection on a potential future,
has forced me to dredge up things that I had buried deep. These
things are feelings of pain. In the extreme. They are things that
made me question myself and the very essence of who I am. They
are things retold now as stories with a humorous, cavalier twist,
but, in truth, they are stories of the darkest time of my life.

It doesn't matter how much you mentally prepare yourself for
motherhood, nothing prepares you for the first three months. No
matter how many books you read or how many friends you ask or
how many times you consult Doctor Google, you can never really

know. In retrospect, I realise that there is little point in reading those books at all because you can't really remember anything in the initial six to twelve weeks.

It's all a blur of pain, anxiety, self-loathing, self-questioning and guilt. Oh, the guilt. Guilt that is internalised, social- ised, culturally propagated and even embedded in our medical institutions. And while I have few clear recollections of new motherhood, what little I do remember is vividly etched in my brain. There are flashes of painful memory, slivers of time that stuck when the rest of it washed away.

There are moments in time that are with you forever, you see.

Like the day when I almost lost my life.

The birth of my son was swift but difficult. I had an allergic reac- tion to the induction gel and, whoosh, there is no time for an epidural now, my dear. (A word to the wise: ask for the epidural *straightaway*.) I remember that straight after he was born, my first thoughts were pure panic. Urgently, I asked if the baby was okay. Yes, yes, I was assured. A healthy boy, followed by cups of tea, vegemite toast, love and warmth from partner and mum.

Then peaceful sleep, or so I thought.

Hours later, I was standing, hovered over the ensuite toilet in my hospital room looking at Trevor. Our baby, our peanut, is warm and safe in his embrace, but Trevor's face is washed grey and his panic-stricken eyes are screaming wordlessly at me *Don't die.* There is blood everywhere and eventually I pass out. I find out later that I had a massive haemorrhage. This happens sometimes. Apparently. I've lived to tell the tale.

———

I remember going home with our peanut. I can still see him, so small in that safety seat, still screaming and crying, but, hey, you're going home. Oh fuck, you are going home . . .

———

Sleep! The baby won't sleep. He's hungry. So feed him. You must breastfeed! But I'm exhausted. No milk. None. None at all. Please give him a 'supplementary' feed. Fine, but you must breast-feed. That's natural. Wait. No milk. The baby screams. No milk. Guilt. Try again. It's natural. I'm tired. He's hungry. Please help. You need to try breastfeeding. It's natural. Baby screams. Again. No sleep.

———

I go to the doctor and little peanut is underweight. This is noth-ing to worry about. Yet. But still come the questions: Are you breastfeeding? No. Well, with the haemorrhage and the subse-quent iron tablets you're not producing milk properly so how could you? But are you breastfeeding? It's what's best. It's natural. You need to try breastfeeding. You are also constipated, which is awesome. Have you tried breastfeeding?

———

Fuck breastfeeding. If it's not working for you, if you are liter-ally not producing milk, or not coping, fuck the guilt, feed your child. No guilt. Not any more. Breathe, it's all good, just breathe. Get used to whispering *What the fuck* and *For fuck's sake* loudly and ad nauseum.

———

You thought your experience at hospital was bad? Sister, strap yourself in 'cause you ain't seen nothing yet. You are battered and bruised, your body is not what it used to be, you can't even com-prehend what's just happened to your vagina. Your boobs don't work (they're not natural, you see) and you're dead tired. But this is nothing compared to what your brain is about to do.

_____

See, you didn't get a 'Good One'. Darling peanut is colicky and cranky and just doesn't sleep. Maybe forty-five minutes maximum on each occasion. So you pace and rock, you are singing till you're hoarse. You lullaby and pet and pat and swing. GO THE FUCK TO SLEEP, you think, you whisper, you say, you scream. You sob, a lot.

I remember sitting on the couch and my darling boy (AKA terrorist) was screaming again and I was crying again. Mum was there, she was always there to lend a helping hand, and all I could do was sob. Sobbing with frustration. Sobbing with hate. Sobbing with guilt. Sobbing with loathing. Please, help me to help you, they say. Please stop crying, you think about both yourself and the baby. Please, please, please.

_____

How the fuck did I end up like this? Me? The proud, strong and career-driven unionist who loves her job and has a passion. How did I go from driving a strategy, from setting a political agenda, to sobbing on the couch with no control over my life, my emotions or my decisions? How is it that I can be surrounded by my caring collective and yet remain alone and isolated? How did I end up beholden to a screaming terrorist (AKA darling boy) and the demons that have emerged in my head?

_____

Be warned, those demons are fuckers.

_____

God damn it, I bloody knew it. I knew that motherhood was not for me. How could you be so selfish as to have a child when you knew that you wouldn't be any good at caring for it? How could you be already thinking about going back to work? How could you want to leave him?

Bruised and battered as you were, the truth is you would've taken anything. Any alternative was better than the nightmare you were living.

I hated myself and I hated my child. I hated my partner, my life, and it felt as if this horror show, which I enthusiastically signed up for, would go on forever. In the middle of the screaming tsunami that never seemed to end, I thought about punting my darling peanut out the window. I've never played AFL, but that's the picture that was in my head nonetheless.

In actual fact, none of those things, none of those feelings, were really me.

That was Postnatal Depression.

Outrageously, it's not until writing this letter to my former self that I've bothered to look up the symptoms and to understand this disease. To name it for what it was. Reviewing the list, the truth of what I went through becomes clear: common symptoms including a low mood; being unable to sleep; feeling inadequate, like a failure, guilty, ashamed, worthless, hopeless, close to tears, angry or irritable; and feeling afraid – afraid of being alone or that you might harm yourself or your baby.

I knew at the time I wasn't me, but being a proud, strong and stubborn soul, I persisted in spite of it. I was scared and that is so outrageous. I want to shout at myself to get help. I ruined my mental health and I threatened my relationship with a supportive, loving partner. I will now live with the guilt and scars of that experience forever.

I have no memory of joyfully holding my newborn son. I have no memories of feeling maternal, the way I do now, about him. I wish I could recall comforting him without sobbing myself. I wish I could recall tending to his early needs without pain and guilt.

My son is my everything and I reckon he always has been, only it was shaded with grey for a while. I wasn't always that way, clouded in the shrouds of depression, and I hope that is not my future. It could have been easier if only I had checked myself and asked for help, and that is my wish for any other new mother who feels the way I did. I wish for them to know that it's not their fault, that they don't have to be scared, that they can ask for help and find it. It could have been better for me, if only I had found a way to ask.

Breathe. It's all good, just breathe.

Love,
Kara

Alissa Warren

'This tiny, screaming, mustard-coloured-pooping bundle who has turned your life into a pavlova, is going to be your pathway to more friendships.'

Dear Alissa,

Pavlova. In those newborn weeks, life is a little like a pavlova.

It can be heaven: perfect, sweet-as and wonderfully surprising. It can also be disastrous, over-the-top and not nearly as great as it looks from the outside. But there is one element of the pavlova that will always carry it through. One ingredient that – if picked perfectly – will make a pavlova shine. It is the hero of your dish. It is the hero of your life.

The fruit.

Your girlfriends.

Yep. Indeedy. A smattering of strawberries, a few juicy kiwis, a bit of a random orange, some loose bitter blueberries and a pop of passionfruit. Every piece – every friend – is gloriously different. Every piece – every friend – is wholly needed.

Girlfriends come in every shape, size and taste. There's the ever-reliable childhood friend, a friendship based on time and understanding. There's the loopy girlfriend you can't live without but you can't live with. There's the work wife who got you through endless days with your psychopathic boss and the WAGs who learn to love you for everything you are. There's the friend who just gets you.

These are the women who will turn your life into a five-star, three-hatted restaurant during what is a major renovation crisis. They are the fruit on your pavlova. Good fruit can make a shitty pavlova sing.

Beyond the steady, loving presence of your girlfriends, life with a newborn is completely unpredictable. Fun, hard, crazy, complicated. And no matter how many times you do it (that will end up being FOUR times for you, my dear) it's always a challenge.

It is your girlfriends – the women in your life – who have got you through motherhood so far and will continue to way into the future. Through the newborn bit, the toddler bit, the school bit and, one day, I have no doubt, it'll be these same women (hopefully plus a few more) who will carry me through the cranky teenager bit.

During those newborn weeks of motherhood, it is the important and *unexpectedly* important women in your life who will carry you. Actress Kate Hudson once said:

We had this bridal shower for my sister-in-law, and my mom made this speech, and she said, 'I want all the girls to look around the room and, even if you don't know each other, even if you're just getting to know each other, or even if it's your sister, I want you to remember one thing: trust me. Men, they come and go. They always will. Hopefully, they stay. But, it's the girl that's sitting next to you, or the girl that's sitting across from you, that's going to get you through everything.

Firstly, beyond cool. A bridal shower with Goldie Hawn and Kate Hudson. Secondly, Goldie Hawn seems to know a little about love. Particularly, the special kind of love between friends.

I know you're inevitably going to start feeling guilty now. You'll think about how rarely you organise to catch up with your girlfriends and how you need to be better and how you're just so busy and – STOP IT, ALISSA.

That stuff is inevitable. Distance and time are depressing, but also painfully normal. The fact you don't see each other often enough makes those rare moments all the sweeter. Different girlfriends will show up at just the right time or in just the right place. Sometimes – and quite often it's the case – it's the person you least expect who saves you.

After the arrival of my first baby, I had a girlfriend walk with me. Nearly every day we walked to the shops to buy some lentils, some baking paper, some lip balm or something I probably didn't really need. (I'll be honest, at any given time I have about eight half-used lip balms floating around in the bottom of my handbag.)

But that daily walk gave me purpose – purpose beyond the relentless cycle of feeding, changing and soothing the baby. Sometimes she'd push the pram if I could take the control-freak setting down a notch. (Alissa, you're going to be obsessed with seventeen-minute interval feeding, controlled crying remedies and endless other rules for baby number one. Don't worry, it passes for the second and is non-existent for the third and fourth.)

Sometimes we walked for hours and sometimes just minutes.

But we went. Every. Single. Day.

And then, with time, came the point where I no longer needed to walk every day. I couldn't walk every day. There was work, play dates, appointments, playgroup, the gym, and sometimes I just needed a day to myself. The walk departed, but the friendship remained. Strengthened, even. She had walked me through when I most needed it. Like always, friendships and rituals can morph, change, blossom and sleep.

Back to my pavlova. Yum.

Different types for different times, right? Sometimes it just needs to be topped with a mountain of strawberries. Donna-Hay style. No blueberries. No kiwi. No orange or whatever. Maybe just a taste of passionfruit. But strawberries might be all you need and all you want.

My strawberry walking friend was all I needed and I was on a high dose. It was plentiful, fulfilling, reliable. Simple. It has always been that way. She's always been the mainstay. Every pavlova needs strawberries, right? And that was okay. More than okay. It was perfect. Because all the other fruit was in short supply, out of season, overpriced or just not available for whatever reason.

In those first few weeks of having a baby, this can be the hardest thing about topping your pavlova. What you think you're hungry for changes. What you expect to receive isn't always dished up on your plate.

Before my little bundle of joy arrived and threw a bomb under my previously very manageable life, I had a set of expectations about who would be there for me. I thought I knew exactly which friends would be there for the sporadic phone calls, the complaints about my lack of sleep and endless loads of washing, to understand the longing to reclaim my life and the quest to still 'be me'.

I was wrong.

Maybe they were working.

Maybe they had kids of their own.

Maybe they just didn't get it.

This was a surprise. The arrival of a baby will give your friendships a good shake and a big shock. Some friendships will come out stronger than ever before and some will disappear. Most just change. Because some people will understand what you're going through right now and some won't for a very long time. Some never will. Some simply forget.

Like every event – finishing school, moving out of home, finding love, the death of a family member, a new job or getting married – having a baby tests your friendships. It tests you. A new mother isn't faultless herself. Sometimes the absolute crappest friend is a new mother. You might be distracted, tired, overwhelmed, tired, coping, tired, not coping and tired. Tired. Did I mention you'd be tired?

But a new mother needs her friends most of all.

Her friends are the magic.

Alissa, in what feels like the most godforsaken mess right now, friends will appear when you least expect it. And they will again and again. With each new baby will come a beautiful new friend, or remade friend or renewed friend or more resilient friend.

After the arrival of your second baby, a girlfriend will pop in unannounced before work. Not a lick of make-up, wearing Dunlop trainers and carrying a brick-sized banana cake. This friend is not a pop-in friend. She has three kids of her own, lives on the other side of town and works full-time. She's the busiest friend you have, but she knew from your text chat she should probably check in.

Four years on, you'll finally thank her for that morning and ask her why she popped in during a time when life was just as busy for her. She will respond by saying that, 'You sounded flat so I was just dropping in to make sure you weren't postnatal. Turns out you were just tired.'

On that day, she will be your little piece of orange atop that messy, exhausted half-baked mess of a pavlova. An unexpected but very welcome addition to your mummy life, arriving when you least expected it and most needed it. Perfection.

Friendships will surprise you during these first few weeks.

And the best bit? It only gets more delicious.

Having this baby means at some stage, you'll be forced to make new friends. Mothers' group, pre-school, school. Out there, there are friends you don't even know yet. I hope that gives you a whole lot of warm-fuzzies, because it should. In this very moment when you feel alone and isolated, dear friends of your future are somewhere in the country doing exactly what you are. They are comforting and nursing and sleeping. Well, actually, they're probably not sleeping.

You'll meet those fruity friends in the most unlikely places, perhaps crying at the local chemist during your baby's twelve-week check-up because they haven't put on two hundred grams. Or moaning on the sidelines at a basketball game because it's way too bloody early to be rolling out of bed to watch your now seven-year-old flop around the court.

Or at the beach, because your three-year-old is playing mermaids in the water with another girl and, as it turns out, her mum is quite a hoot and she may also have a bottle of wine and an extra plastic cup in her beach bag.

Alissa, no matter how perfect or how disastrous each pavlova is, if you focus on the fruit then you're going to be okay. These newborn weeks are scary and daunting, but they are also precious. After all, the joy comes not only in the eating, but in that moment the piece of cake is flopped onto your plate.

If you start with your girlfriends – no matter how close, how reliable, how understanding, how predictable – things will work out. It's those friendships, those fleeting moments of support, that'll reignite the fire in your belly. Or, better still, the love in your heart. The love for yourself, for your new baby and for life.

It truly is the ultimate gift: a friend. And this tiny, screaming, mustard-coloured-pooping bundle who has turned your life into a pavlova, is going to be your pathway to more friendships. Your little baby is to give you some of the greatest moments of your life. And, best of all, friendships you never thought you needed.

And I think that's worth getting up in the morning for. At 2 a.m. And 3 a.m. And 4 a.m. And 5 a.m. Oh, and 6 a.m.

Good morning and good luck.

Alissa

Clare O'Neil

*'I promised no advice but I do have a request. Please take the
to-do list that you wrote when you went on maternity leave
(learn to paint, take up yoga, surfing, write a book . . . seriously?),
screw it up into a ball and throw it straight in the bin.'*

Dear Clare,

In the past six weeks, you have been pooed, splattered, dripped,
spewed and wee'd on. You haven't slept more than three hours in a
row for two months. You have discovered an emotional range you
previously weren't aware of, experiencing wild euphoria and utter
misery at exactly the same time. Chaos has reigned; a clean house
in the morning, strewn with baby paraphernalia by lunchtime.
And you have survived this, the most challenging time in the life
of your little baby.

New mums get so much advice: much of it contradictory,
little of it genuinely helpful. Go to him when he cries, don't go
to him. Feed him whenever he wants, feed him every four hours.

Hold him like this, no, like that. I'm not going to add to the problem by filling this letter with more.

Instead, I want you to know that it is all about to get easier. Soon you will have a day where bub naps for the recommended three hours. You will have time for a shower, a coffee, some exercise. Breastfeeding will get easier and you won't even remember all the tears and heartache it took to get there. Pretty soon, you'll start to feel normal again.

Some moments over the last six weeks have felt terribly dark. A bad feed, a day when bub won't sleep a single wink, times when you're upset, or fighting with your partner. Often you wake with a surge of energy and a sense of promise only to feel utterly defeated an hour later.

Good parenting isn't about what happens in these moments. It's not the grumpy outburst or terribly crap day that matters. It's the big stuff that counts: loving your child, nurturing your relationship, being there for your family.

I know that for sure because, three years on, Clare, you have two beautiful, happy boys. One is a new baby, a sweet lamb with perfect soft skin and a smell you get utterly lost in. The other is a big, independent and energetic three-year-old, who loves Spiderman and dinosaurs and collecting rocks, who climbs trees, begs for ice cream and shrieks with excitement when he finds ants in the sandpit. Who, every night after his bath, covers his head with a towel and pretends to be a ghost. A boy with his own little life and friends and hobbies.

This moment, when you are all that matters to your child, will pass very quickly. While it may be hard to see through the sandpapery half-opened slits with which you currently view the world, among the tough stuff and difficulties of these first months, there is also indescribable joy. The deep love you feel, the uncomplicated devotion, your limitless drive to meet the every need of this child. The flood of elation you feel when baby smiles, gurgles and laughs. It is full-intensity living and it is beautiful.

I promised no advice but I do have a request. Please take the to-do list that you wrote when you went on maternity leave (learn to paint, take up yoga, surfing, write a book . . . seriously?), screw it up into a ball and throw it straight in the bin.

All that matters right now – your only job – is to live in this moment. Stare at baby's little fingers and toes. Stroke his beautiful head. Lie on the ground next to him. Talk to him, and give him plenty of time to share his thoughts and feelings on the day. Sing to him. Smell his special smell. Grin stupidly. Cuddle.

I want you to cherish this moment because it's going to be over much sooner than you think. The months you thought you'd have to devote to this time of your life are about to come to a dramatic close.

Bub has been born in the middle of a federal election campaign. That might not seem like a big deal to most, but for you it's going to matter enormously. Politics has been your passion for your whole life. This election is the first you can remember that you haven't been obsessively working on or following, as you've been too busy fretting about labour, wiping poo off your arm and feeling guilty about not doing your pelvic floor exercises.

One evening soon you're going to get a flood of phone calls from people who want you to run for parliament. The electorate where you were previously mayor, the region where you lived and worked and studied and volunteered over many years, needs a new representative. The calls will come only three weeks away from election day. If you agree to run for parliament, you'll be on the campaign trail immediately. If you win, you'll be an MP within a month, heading to Canberra with an eleven-week old baby.

Some people who run for election are blissfully ignorant as to what it entails. That's not you. You've seen it up close. It's utterly gruelling. If you sign on, you'll be away from your family for more than a third of the year, every year, living a life of constant, impossibly heartbreaking choices between work and family. It's missed birthdays and parent-teacher interviews and school concerts. It's Sunday morning phone calls and waking at 4 a.m. to rush to the airport. It's immense responsibility and stress, a constant feeling of debt to friends and family, and guilt at never being the mother, partner, friend, sister that you want to be.

But, you also know the truth about politics. Politics gets bad press. From a distance, all people see is the conflict and combat, the political games. But up close, it is deeply meaningful and inspiring. Politics can, and frequently does, improve the lives of millions of people.

You think about the people you have known who desperately need change to be made. The Indigenous families you worked with when you lived in Arnhem Land – who lived ten-people to a two-bedroom household, who had lost hope that government would ever be there for them, if they ever believed it to begin with.

You think about the farmers in your family, who do back-breaking work every day but still struggle to survive, and the rural communities they love that are in decay. The young girls you meet who already believe their value lies in their appearance. The baby you fostered, and how she deserves a chance at living a better life than her parents. In politics, you will have the power to do something to help them.

And then you look down at the little baby in your arms.

There is no more obvious responsibility, none that you could feel more instinctively, than to look after this child. It's one thing to go down a political path with teenagers, or kids in primary school. But how could you possibly make that choice when you are responsible for a being so helpless he cannot sit up or crawl, who depends on you fully and completely just to keep living?

The night you agree to take the plunge, you will not sleep, not for a single second. Your mind is full of fear and uncertainty, of guilt, of confusion. All you can think of is how this decision will affect your new baby boy.

The next day, exhausted and with an eight-week-old baby strapped to your chest, you drag on the work clothes that have been stored in the bottom of the cupboard and you hit the campaign trail. Knocking on doors. Talking to journalists. Manning street stalls. Speaking to voters. Three weeks later, you're elected to parliament – an unbelievable privilege, a chance to do something good, something big, something real.

The reality of being a politician and having young children is exactly as good and as bad as you thought it would be. Sometimes you will kiss your family goodbye and cry all the way to the airport. Frequently, you will sit in Question Time while scores of angry middle-aged men yell indiscriminately in your direction and wonder what on earth you were thinking. You also get to fight every day for things you care about, and stand up for people who need strong advocates.

The thing that makes all this possible is the person you have chosen to share your life with. One of the biggest challenges to getting equality for women is getting men to step up. Plenty of fellas say all the right things, but it takes a real man to do what it takes – to put aspects of their career on hold, to get their hands dirty with extra childcare and chores, to genuinely relish the success of their partner – to support a woman in politics. The more I get on, the more I realise, Clare, how big you got lucky.

And with a lot of extra support from parents, in-laws, aunties, friends, and everyone in between, you will be able to make these two very important jobs, of being an MP and a mum, work together. An office strewn with baby wraps and children's toys, a cot and change table in Canberra, a little one crawling under your desk during meetings, a baby being loved and cuddled by your colleagues on the floor of parliament.

But that's all in the future.

Clare, you've got two weeks left to be the type of parent you always wanted to be. Give yourself permission to get wholly and completely lost in the child you adore more than anything in the world. Even at your lowest, even through the occasional bouts of tears, you are aware of the deep joy of caring for and loving that child. Feel it. Hold onto it. Treasure it. Relish it and savour every last second.

Three years along, you will not dwell on the bad times, the chaos, the frustrations and disappointments and stresses. Instead, you will simply remember this, the briefest of moments, when all that mattered in the world was the beautiful baby boy you are holding in your arms.

With love,
Clare

Holly Wainwright

'For you right now, "night" just means doing the same thing you've been doing all day but quietly, in the dark, with more anxiety. So let's talk about that part, the anxious part. Hopefully, I can help with that.'

Dear Me,

I know about the photos.

So just cry, go on. It's brutal. I know.

Let those tears pour, let the snot bubble, let the sobs choke your throat.

It's been seven years this week, and ever-helpful Facebook is reminding me of my first months as a mother. And those photos show an idyllic time.

There's Matilda in that purple cotton singlet you love so much, fast asleep on her daddy's chest, a tiny bare arm flung above her head. There she is again curled into a papoose on his chest, walking the cliff path to ease her off to sleep. Wow. What an amazing dad.

There's the family out to brunch, the pram barely in frame, hot coffees and smashed eggs, newspapers on the table. That photo has a lot to say. Look at us, doing all the things! Look at us, everything's just the same! Look at us, living the dream!

And there you are smiling at the camera, newborn Matilda in your arms. There's a look on your face that's familiar. A textbook study of adoration. It's beautiful to see, the way you are looking at your baby. You can see the circles under your eyes and no fear visible behind them.

But I know the truth about the photos.

I know about all the photos you didn't take. The scenes of early motherhood you didn't capture. The ones you didn't parade on social media. The ones that wouldn't have garnered a flood of likes and comments and heart-eyed emojis.

Like the one of you sitting up in bed at night, sobbing, breasts exposed, nipples raw and bleeding.

Or the one of you thrusting your baby towards her amazing dad and saying, 'You take her, I just can't. I just can't. I just can't.' Over and over.

The one of that brunch, the coffee cold, the eggs congealed, untouched on their hipster slates, the baby squalling, other diners scowling.

No Instagram filter can disguise the time you walked out of the house and kept walking. You walked and walked and wanted to walk and walk and walk away from this new life that you didn't recognise and never return.

I know about the photos and it's okay.

Because this time is brutal.

Right now, you're a little bit furious at everyone who didn't tell you that looking after a tiny person is much, much more difficult than it looks. You're also a little bit furious at yourself about all the people who did tell you that but you didn't believe.

They should have taken you by the shoulders and shaken you. They should have encouraged you to get a tattoo on the inside of your wrist that reads: *Your name is Holly Wainwright. You live in Sydney, Australia. You have a functioning brain. You've done a lot of stuff. People generally think you're all right. You will survive this. Probably . . .*

Tiny writing in a tasteful spiral. Obviously.

You are looking at everyone – strangers in the street, treasured friends, *your own parents* – and you're thinking: 'You have done this before. You have taken a tiny child home from a hospital. You have tried to decipher its mysterious signals. You have tried to fulfil its many wants and needs. You have tried so hard to keep it alive that you have barely remembered to do the same for yourself. You have done this. WHY DIDN'T YOU TELL ME?'

I know. It's brutal.

Because now you're beginning to suspect it's not them, it's you. Clearly everyone else – those shiny-haired mothers in the nappy commercials, those women jogging with prams along the beachfront, those ab-tastic bitches on Instagram – are breezing through motherhood. It's just you who is sitting on the couch, trying to breastfeed and guilt-crying through the entire back catalogue of *Mad Men*.

You think it's just you who's finding solace in epic amounts of banana bread, and the glass of wine you shouldn't be having every night.

Luckily, I'm here with hindsight from the future and I have something comforting to tell you: It's not just you. Nobody is good at this first part. Nobody is even good at listening to the advice about the first part.

Remember the midwife in your prenatal class? Remember how she tried to warn you about the strange warping of time and space that new motherhood brings? She ran the intensive courses – the one you went to two Saturday mornings in a row because, really, who has the time? (You think you didn't have time. You will discover, in the coming years, that you had all the time in the world.)

That woman was lovely, with a warm smile and sensible hair and comfortable shoes and the kind of calm, understated demeanour that allows people in her profession to use the word 'discomfort' when they're describing labour pain.

At lunchtime her husband brought their eighteen-month-old to the hospital to be breastfed. You thought, 'Gosh, don't parents make a fuss. She seems so sensible, and there she is, interrupting her work to feed her baby.' You had a lot to learn, Old Me. You still do.

The bit you didn't get was this: 'It comes as quite a shock that looking after Baby' – every new life is just Baby, every new mum is just Mum – 'is a 24-hour-a-day job. Mum often finds that on a feeding schedule, day and night don't quite have the same distinction as they did before Baby.'

A 24-hour-a-day job. The couples in that room didn't realise what the nice lady with the warm smile was trying to tell them. They just kept smiling and nodding. The women kept rubbing their ever-expanding ankles. The men – in at least one case – kept on snoring, quietly.

And that's what's really hitting you right now. The 24-hour-a-day part.

Matilda is a peach of a baby – pink and gold and lightly fuzzed, sweet-smelling, delicious – but she wakes at least every three hours, night or day. And you are feeding her. And your nipples can't handle the demand, and they hurt, and you scream internally every time she latches on.

It's brutal. I know.

Just scream, Holly. Nobody is about to present you with a medal for stoicism. Pretending this isn't difficult is what got everyone into this mess in the first place.

So there's the nipples. And the 24-hour shock. And the night terrors.

Not Matilda's. Yours.

You're doing a pretty good job of staying optimistic in the 'morning's but the late afternoons are killing you. As the realisation dawns that another night is coming, and for you there will be no rest, you're finding it hard to keep it together. There's a welling sense of dread.

For you right now, 'night' just means doing the same thing you've been doing all day but quietly, in the dark, with more anxiety. So let's talk about that part, the anxious part. Hopefully, I can help with that.

Holly, you are not a bad mother because you're not loving every moment of this. You are not a bad mother because you're hiding from well-meaning visitors in the bathroom, incapable of making small talk and smiling. You are not a bad mother because sometimes, when Matilda cries as your head hits the pillow, you swear and curse and grab her from the crib a little more roughly than you ever would in those Facebook videos.

You don't realise this yet, but you're going to be a great mother.

You already are, and you will continue to be.

Not because your baby sleeps through the night (I really don't want to alarm you, or encourage you to postpone marital relations indefinitely, but if you think this baby is a bad sleeper, wait until you meet your next one), or because your kids always look immaculate, or because you mush your own organic baby food (you will manage that a total of about three times during two different weening phases, GO YOU). It's not because you are the woman who will finally master work-life balance, or the one who never, ever hands her toddler the phone when you're talking to the woman in the post office.

Nope. That's not you.

But you are a good mum, because that little peach-person loves you to pieces. And you do her. You're only going to love each other more, and more, and more. And with that locked in, the rest is really just window dressing.

See what I did there, Old Me? I threw you a bone. I gave you a glimmer of hope to help you through the twilight zone of this strange opposite world where there is no day or night, and where you doubt you will ever feel human again.

It's brutal. I know.

And here you are, crying again. Exhaustion will do that to you. The tiredness that seems to seep into your very bone marrow, that mingles with your DNA, that has you marvelling at how you can still move your arms and legs, at how you can still make your mouth form words . . .

Enough waffling. Enough. What's the point of a letter from the future unless it's actually going to be useful? Let me tell you what I've learned . . .

Go to mothers' group: I know that involves brushing your hair and putting on clothes that aren't pyjama pants, but, truly, it's the best thing you can do for yourself and for Matilda. The Best. At mothers' group you will learn, almost immediately, that everyone is in exactly the same mess you are.

No one's baby is sleeping through the night. (I'm actually laughing as I write that, as if that's actually a possibility in the first six weeks, as if anyone should have ever suggested that it might be, you know, A Thing.)

None of those women have any idea why your baby suddenly just starts crying at 4 p.m. for no reason at all. They are also clueless about why she just keeps whingeing until 6 p.m. and refuses to be put down, something that is completely incompatible with the other things you're meant to be doing at that time of day, like, you know, making a meal. (I'm laughing again.)

These excellent women will become your friends. They will save your sanity, over and over. Together, you will try everything and exchange all of the information. Day sleeps – why are they so impossible? Is there such a thing as 'bedtime' for a newborn?

Should you rock and pat, or just shush? Should you bounce up and down on a fitness ball? Should you drive around and around at 2 a.m. when you've exhausted all other options? None of you have any idea, but having people to text swear words to at 11 p.m. will make you feel a whole lot better.

So brush your hair and get out the door.

Stop tiptoeing around at night: You know how Matilda wakes up every couple of hours and you carry her carefully away from where she's sleeping next to your bed and into her 'nursery' where you change her and feed her and basically make sure that she goes from really, really sleepy to really, really awake? Stop doing that. Just stop.

You claim you don't want to wake Brent, but it's a ridiculous, passive-aggressive farce. He can hear her crying. He can hear you thudding around. You're not fooling anyone. Just do everything right there, in your bed, preferably without putting your feet on the floor. Yes, he has to go to work in the morning. So what? So do you. This baby business isn't work?

This is a team sport. You're lucky enough to be in a team of three so make the most of it. Brent can learn to change nappies in the dark too, you know. It's not a skill that comes with having a uterus.

Enjoy it: I know you are spitting at Future Me right now. I know you just ripped this missive from the future into tiny shreds and added it to the bonfire of your workplace, but seriously, if you could see the next seven years you would know how unique this very ordinary experience is.

You will never again be a first-time mother getting to know your oldest child. You will never again be on such a ridiculously steep learning curve. You will never again have the time, the time, the TIME, to focus on one job the way you are focusing on keeping that little peach-person alive right now.

That baby is seven years old now. She's tall and strong, and she likes to sleep next to you, she likes to lie there and tell you all her stories, hear all of yours. She's funny, and she's kind and brave. She's big sister to a whirlwind and she adores her dad.

She doesn't give a shit about you watching *Mad Men* while you breastfed. She doesn't remember that you flayed your nipples for her. She still doesn't really let you sit and enjoy hot coffee and smashed eggs at a cafe.

But she adores you.

And you're building that future relationship right now.

Holly, that overwhelming fear welling inside you is absolutely correct: Life is never going to be the same again. It's going to be way, way better than that. So cry. Cry it out.

Because it's brutal. I know.

Brutally beautiful.

Me x

Clare Bowditch

*'The answer is, yes. Motherhood is your watershed. This will
be your awakening. This is the day you realise who you
are and who you will go on to be: a fighter.'*

Listen, darling,

I don't want you to take this the wrong way but basically – *it's all
over for you.*

Here you are, late in the night on the day after the day after
the day you gave birth. You gave flaming violent glorious birth to a
seven pound baby daughter who will barely sleep but will also barely
cry and now you're home again, home again, finally home again.

You are just about to lower your swollen sack of womanhood
down into the water of your very own bathtub, but you're hes-
itating because you're scared of the pain that might follow; of
what will happen when those two new stitches holding together
the place where your vagina used to be touch the hot water. Your

arms are holding your body weight on the sides of the tub, new muscles already forming, and your neck is stretching upwards. You're too scared to look down.

Slowly now. Slowly. Take your time, Bowditch.

In a moment you will have eased your way down into that water and feel the glorious relief, that same glorious relief you experienced days earlier when, in the impossibility of labour, your boyfriend and best friend donned rubber gloves and tongs and dunked cloth nappies into a hot bucket of water and slapped those hot cloth nappies one after the other on the small of your back where it ached that ache that a hundred billion women before you have felt. In that moment you remembered them all, felt connected to them all.

You called on them, the women who went before, as your baby was crowning, as your best friend promised, 'Keep going! You will hold your baby soon!' And you did. Right there you held the entire perfection of her, a beautiful bread-dough of life, fully formed, using her lily white elbows to grunt and drag her way straight up your stomach and latch onto your dark-brown bullseye of an areola for the first time.

These new memories flash across your mind right now as you close your eyes during that first ever bath as a new mother, which also happens to coincide with your first moment of being truly alone in . . . you try to calculate in your head: thirty, sixty, ninety . . . hundreds of days straight. You no longer share your body with another. And here you are, home again, everyone safe and you did it.

You broke free from that overcrowded public hospital ward, where the midwives were so incredibly tender that it only made the cruelty of The One Mean Nurse that much harsher. The One

Mean Nurse who would not, I repeat NOT, let you go home and laughed at you when you refused to hand over your baby to go to the nursery.

The one who, just as your boyfriend lay down beside you with your daughter between you on the bed for your first moment together as an actual family, ripped open the flimsy hospital bed-curtain with such violence that you jumped. You woke the baby, who cried, and the nurse scoffed at your boyfriend for having the *gumption* to lie down beside his loved ones, saying, 'Get up! This isn't your bed!'

There you were, raw as silk, messy as melting ice, turning to liquid once more. You started crying along with your daughter, begging the nurse to please let you go home now, whimpering, 'Please, I need to go home. I can't sleep with six other new mothers and new babies in the room. I need to go home.' She rolls her eyes and tells you to stop being so silly, as though you know nothing of your own needs.

She has refused for twenty-four hours now because she reckons your daughter hasn't wee-wee'd yet, and you're trying so hard to speak with dignity but the ancient instinct to fight is so strong that a new voice is born in you, declaring a truth you never thought you'd be so desperate to speak. You say, 'SHE *HAS* WEE-WEE'D! SHE WEE-WEE'D AS SOON AS SHE CAME OUT! ON *ME*! I REMEMBER!'

The One Mean Nurse's attitude is 'Well, I didn't see it, so I'm afraid it doesn't count,' and you look at her, a grown woman who should really know better than this. You wonder if perhaps she has been treating the other women in this ward the same way she is treating you now and has perhaps been getting away with it for decades.

To be so careless with women at their most vulnerable should be criminal. Every smell, sight, sound, feeling is so incredibly amplified. In those first tender moments of your forever-walk into motherhood, what you need more than anything is a sliver of true kindness.

And with this one clear thought, it is as if something crisp inside of you snaps. A capsule of righteousness is released and new strength rolls into you and you hear a noise then, your own throat making a noise like a low grown from a tigress defending her ground.

You breathe in, swallow, your sobbing stops, a tone of steel creeps into your voice, and you make it known, very clearly and in no uncertain terms, using your new voice, that your husband is not going anywhere, because he is here to collect you, because you will be going home. Today. With your baby. So she had better hurry up and kindly sign those papers, which she refuses to do, again.

You call her bluff; you call the Head Doctor Man, a person whose title you have never needed to know before this moment, and when he comes, finally, you state your case and say, 'Please let us go HOME.' The Head Doctor Man agrees that, yes, this is all a bit silly, he's not sure why you're still here, it's marked clearly in your notes that your daughter did indeed poo already, and it's likely you're telling the truth about 'the wee-wee'.

Thank you. Thank you.

You head off, with such relief, with the joy of knowing you have the right once again to self-determine, that sovereignty over your body is yours. You walk, proudly at first but then slowly, slower, very slow indeed, especially now you are around the corner and out of sight of The One Mean Nurse. Now you are shuffling, legs apart, quick in-breaths to allay the pain of the swollen places, and your boyfriend who has the baby in his arms is well up ahead of you.

It's not quite morning yet. It's still dark outside and when you look from the window onto the street below you are shocked now by the *whoosh* of a new terror, a protective, instinctive terror. There is a new knowledge that you must, at all costs, protect this child who walks with her father ahead of you. It is a feeling that is too much to take in all in one bite.

Quickly now, you shuffle into the elevator, looking down at the place on your body where your baby once was, a place that's now soft like jelly in silicone casing, a softness that you will battle with in the months to come. The elevator stops, the automatic doors open and you exit the building, a cool fresh gust of morning wind lifting your hair and you reach to cover your daughter with her blanket, but your boyfriend is on to it and will be 'on to it', thank Christ, forever more.

There is your car waiting for you, which he parked on the street right out the front. You joke that this daughter deserves a white horse-drawn carriage but will have to make do with this old burgundy Falcon, this 'only car you could afford' even with the baby bonus. You don't know yet, but things will be tight for many years to come because you are artists and, boy oh boy, it's amazing what you can do with an onion and a tomato and a can of beans.

You watch your boyfriend – this beautiful, hopeful, proud, brave new father – as he places your baby daughter into the car seat. As the car starts, your heart races, the terror returns and you ask him not to drive so fast and he says he isn't driving fast. He is driving forty kilometres an hour but you feel the danger of it all.

You feel the speed and the risk and the horror of it all. You wonder, was it always like this in the world? Because it feels different now: deeper, more tender.

When you arrive safely home, your boyfriend takes the baby and you take that much longed for bath. Now here you are, in your bathtub, just lowered down and feeling the warmth of the water and it hits you. Holy fuck, you're an actual mother. How the hell are you going to pull this thing off? With that thought, an enormous whoosh of coldness swirls in your chest, and suddenly you're shaking and you're crying again, which makes no sense, because your dreams have came true.

You forget that you haven't slept in days and days now and that terror is normal and will retreat once you've had some sleep. You reach out of the bath and pick up the big white plastic portable home phone and you know who you have to call, but you keep missing the keys. You hear your sister's voice say 'Hello?'

You're sobbing so much that you can't even talk but she, without missing a beat – a mother of three then – laughs the biggest laugh you've ever heard, and says, 'DARLING! My darling! I was waiting for your call! It's okay! Welcome to Day Four!'

You have no idea what she means.

'It's Day Four. Your milk is coming in, your hormones are going nuts, you haven't slept in days, your vagina hurts, you're wondering what the dickens you've done but, baby girl, this is one of THE HARDEST BITS and you're nearly through it! Get Marty to pour you champagne because YOU HAVE ARRIVED! You're a MUM NOW!' The love in her voice and the confidence of it – that is enough for you. That is all you needed to hear.

So yes, little mother, it is all over for you, and by that I mean that the old life is all over. Your days of being independent, of not needing to ask anyone for help, are over. You will grow to rely on your friends and family and neighbours in a new way – and they on you. This is the only way to survive.

Your days of thinking that one day, if you try hard enough, you might attain perfection are over. You will stumble, much more often than you care to share, and you will get back up every time – because you have to. For her.

Your days of being polite to mean people, of staying quiet when you know someone should speak up, of feeling like you don't know what you were put on this earth for, of wondering if there's anything worth fighting for, worth dying for – that's all over.

The answer is, yes. Motherhood is your watershed. This will be your awakening. This is the day you realise who you are and who you will go on to be: a fighter.

You will never, ever, forget the feeling of vulnerability that came over you after you gave birth. It will never leave you but will, in time, morph into something quite magical. It will be one of your greatest treasures. It is a superpower. It's called empathy.

You will use it every single day from now on.

This empathy is essential because you will meet many a One Mean Nurse in your time. There will be people who, for whatever reason, have forgotten the magic of small acts of kindness but they will by far be in the minority. If you're not feeling that empathy – even for them – it's a sign that you're moving too fast and you need a moment to catch up.

My dear, you will feel pride too, because you're a mother now and being a mother means something. You'd assumed you would be a good enough mother, and you are: you just don't know that yet. You feel like you're failing every day, but you are not failing.

You're learning. This stuff is hard. In order for you to learn to care for your child you will be pushed to the outer limits of what you thought was acceptable, or possible. You will be facedown eating dirt, you will lose your looks and your body shape and your time. All illusions of control will fall away and it will be worth it. All of it.

Spoiler: This will all make more sense one day, trust me.

Strap in for the ride. I'll see you when you get here.

CB xo

Editor's Note

In 2017 I travelled to Bihar, India, with my husband and international aid organisation CARE. Locals call Bihar, which is home to more than 100 million people, the 'Forgotten State'. Much of the population lives below the poverty line, but life is particularly dire for women and girls. Only one in ten women participate in the workforce, the female literacy rate sits at just above fifty per cent, and millions of girls are forced into early marriage.

In Bihar, I witnessed firsthand the kinds of conditions women and girls in the developing world give birth in. I knew it would be confronting. What I did not realise was how utterly dehumanising, degrading and deadly these environments could be. It left me humbled and grateful for the expert care I received when delivering my son in Australia. We are so unbelievably lucky to live in a country where first-class medical care is available to everyone – not just the wealthy few.

Sanitation, hygiene, family planning and newborn care are key focuses for CARE Australia, as is making sure that every girl receives an education. Research shows that when you lift a woman out of poverty, she works to bring her family, and indeed her whole community, with her. Investment that gives girls and women better opportunities in life can change and is changing the world.

With the generous support of its contributors – many of whom refused to be paid for their exquisite writing – I have donated my book advance for *The Motherhood* to CARE Australia. This donation will help CARE continue their important work, improving the status of women in places like Bihar and throughout the developing world. By purchasing a copy of this book, you too are part of this contribution to the global Motherhood.

I sincerely thank you for your generosity.

Resources

You can arrange to see your maternal child health nurse or GP at ANY time. No concern is too small. Making comparisons with friends and relatives is not always helpful, because everyone has a different experience with pregnancy, birthing and post partum. If you're not 100 per cent happy with how things are going, then it warrants discussion. Even if it's just for reassurance. There is always help available at any stage of motherhood.

Here are some resources that you may find useful in the early months with a newborn and beyond.

Australian Breastfeeding Association
https://www.breastfeeding.asn.au
Breastfeeding Helpline: 1800 686 268

Better Health Channel
https://www.betterhealth.vic.gov.au/healthyliving/healthy-pregnancy

beyondblue
https://www.beyondblue.org.au/the-facts/postnatal-depression
1300 22 4636

COPE (Centre of Perinatal Excellence)
http://cope.org.au

Just Speak Up: personal stories about experiencing depression and anxiety around the time of becoming a parent (beyondblue)
https://healthyfamilies.beyondblue.org.au/pregnancy-and-new-parents/just-speak-up

PANDA (Perinatal Anxiety & Depression Australia)
https://www.panda.org.au
1300 726 306

Pregnancy, Birth and Baby
https://www.pregnancybirthbaby.org.au/postnatal-depression
1800 882 436

Raising Children, The Australian Parenting Website
http://raisingchildren.net.au

The Royal Children's Hospital Melbourne, kids health info
https://www.rch.org.au/kidsinfo

The Royal Women's Hospital Victoria, mastitis information

https://www.thewomens.org.au/health-information/
pregnancy-and-birth

Contributors

Zoë Foster Blake

Zoë Foster Blake is the author of eight books, the founder of Go-To skincare and Break-Up Boss, and is a keen writer of third-person biographies.

Clare Bowditch

Clare Bowditch is a musician and writer from Melbourne. She has three children (a teenage daughter and identical twin sons) and one husband, Marty Brown.

Laura Chalmers

Laura Chalmers has been a journalist in Adelaide, Canberra, and now Brisbane, as well as press secretary to former Prime Minister Julia Gillard and Senator Penny Wong. She is currently deputy chief of staff at the *Courier Mail.*

Nicky Champ

Nicky Champ is the editor of Business Chicks, Australia's largest and most influential community for women. She lives in Sydney with her husband and two kids, Amelia and Sam. She hopes to one day get eight hours of consecutive sleep again.

Jen Clark

Jen Clark is principal and design director of Jen Clark Design, a highly successful, award-winning graphic and digital design practice headquartered in Melbourne.

Gorgi Coghlan

Gorgi Coghlan is mum to Molly-Rose, a keen gardener and a passionate advocate for child sexual abuse survivors from her hometown of Ballarat, in Victoria. She has worked in the media for over fifteen years and regularly hosts Network Ten's *The Project*.

Georgina Dent

Georgina Dent is a writer, commentator and editor who is a proud advocate for women.

Katie Dimond

Katie 'Monty' Dimond is a radio presenter and the editor/ director/big arse boss at Show + Tell. She is also a mum to two mini men and excels in the making spanakopita department.

Clementine Ford

Clementine Ford is a Melbourne-based writer and speaker who buys too many clothes. She is the author of bestselling book *Fight Like a Girl.*

Alys Gagnon

Alys Gagnon is a writer and editor for www.kidspot.com.au. She lives in Melbourne with her husband, two children and a cat named Julia Gillard.

Carla Gee

Carla Gee is an Australian writer and content creator, who thrives on creativity and midnight snacks (especially chocolate biscuits). She was born in Sydney and now lives in Canberra with her husband and two children.

Felicity Harley

Felicity Harley's career is a bit like the thrill and randomness of a child's first year of life: eighteen years working for Australia's top-selling women's magazines (*Cosmopolitan, Cleo* and founding editor of *Women's Health*), eight years on TV, one year as editor of whimn.com.au.

Sarah Harris

Sarah Harris is a journalist and TV host at Network Ten. She's also the proud mum of two rascally sons and is working hard to master mental kung fu to beat the bully in her head.

Kirstie Innes-Will

Kirstie Innes-Will is a bibliophile who has worked in publishing for over fifteen years. She is currently Managing Editor at Black Inc., where she works on a wide range of commercial, political and literary nonfiction. She lives in Preston with her partner, Jen, son Max, a cat and a rescue greyhound.

Kara Keys

Kara Keys is a mum, unionist, Aboriginal activist. Descendent of the Yiman–Gangulu peoples of Central Queensland. National Campaign Co-ordinator for the ACTU and soldier for working people in the service of the mighty trade union movement.

Emma Macdonald

Emma Macdonald is a multi-award-winning journalist, speaker and maternal health advocate. After the birth of her second child, she co-founded maternal health charity Send Hope Not Flowers, which operates safe birth programs across six countries in the developing world.

Bronwyn McCahon

Bronwyn McCahon is the former Editor-in-chief of *Dolly* and *Cosmopolitan* magazines and founder of children's label PLAY etc. Bronwyn lives in Bondi Beach with her husband and three children.

Suzannah Bayes Morton

Suzannah Bayes Morton is an actor, performance artist, wasabi enthusiast and owns a bakery cafe. She lives in Sydney with her husband, their five-year-old and a newish set of twin boys.

Clare O'Neil

Clare O'Neil is a Labor frontbencher and the federal MP for Hotham, in Melbourne's south-east. She is a former mayor, a Harvard graduate, a Fulbright Scholar and, most importantly, the mother of two gorgeous boys.

Erin O'Neill

Erin O'Neill lives with her husband and three-year-old son in Melbourne's northern suburbs. After four years, three house moves, a wedding and a baby, Erin recently graduated with her Bachelor of Arts (International Studies) and is looking forward to lots of naps before starting a new policy role at Creative Victoria.

Karen Pickering

Karen Pickering is a feminist organiser and writer based in Melbourne. She was the creator and host of Cherchez la Femme, a co-founder of Girls On Film Festival (GOFF), and the editor of *Doing It*, a collection of sex-positive writing by women. Karen is currently writing a book on menstruation and menopause.

Anna Rose

Anna Rose is an author and campaigner doing what she can to stop damage to our climate. She's the author of *Madlands: A Journey to Change the Mind of a Climate Sceptic*, editor of the cookbook *Planet to Plate*, co-founder of the Australian Youth Climate Coalition and former head of Earth Hour Australia.

Jessica Rudd

Jessica Rudd is the author of *Campaign Ruby* and *Ruby Blues*. She lives in Brisbane with her husband and children.

Em Rusciano

Em Rusciano is a writer, comedian, singer, radio presenter, glittery lunatic, and collector of owl figurines. With her morning breakfast show on Sydney's 2DayFM, her recent biography

Try Hard: Tales from the Life of a Needy Overachiever in bookstores, and live comedy shows regularly touring around the country, she is doing absolutely everything she can to be all up in everyone's grill.

Lanai Scarr

Lanai Scarr is a mum of four kids under the age of four, including triplets. When she is not doing piles of washing or trying to stop her toddler trio from destroying the house she also finds time to earn some money as a senior writer for News Corp Australia.

Janine Shepherd

Janine Shepherd, AM, is an author, speaker and aerobatic pilot. Her TEDx talk, 'A Broken Body isn't a Broken Person', has been viewed by millions. She is the author of six books, the most recent being *Defiant*, which chronicles Janine's extraordinary life.

Rebecca Sparrow

Over the past twenty-five years Bec has worked as a publicist, a magazine editor, a newspaper columnist, a TV scriptwriter and a novelist. She is the author of the bestselling books *Ask Me Anything* and *Find Your Tribe*, co-hosts the award-winning podcast The Well and speaks to thousands of teenagers every year about friendship, resilience and having a more positive experience online.

Jo Stanley

Jo Stanley has done decades of breakfast radio, tonnes of guest roles on TV, written a kids' book series, and sometimes performs live. She is an ambassador for Smiling Mind, because mindfulness makes her much nicer to be around.

Kumi Taguchi

Kumi Taguchi was born in Melbourne to an Australian mother and Japanese father. She has worked in the media for over twenty years. Kumi is a classical violinist, has run a desert marathon and has sailed the Sydney to Hobart. She lives in Sydney with her husband and daughter.

Holly Wainwright

Holly Wainwright is Head of Content at Mamamia.com.au and the author of *The Mummy Bloggers*, a 'darkly hilarious' novel about lives lived online. She's also the host of podcast This Glorious Mess and mum to two small children who miraculously made it through those first chaotic weeks.

Alissa Warren

Alissa Warren is a journalist with fifteen years experience, having worked for *A Current Affair, Nine News* and various online and print publications including *The Sunday Telegraph* and Mamamia. Alissa's also a keen netballer, swimmer and mum to four small children who keep her busy, knackered and gloriously happy.

Nareen Young

Nareen Young is one of Australia's most senior, respected and innovative workplace diversity practitioners. She has been doing this work way before it was sexy, has presented, published and commentated nationally and internationally and has won many awards and accolades, including the Inaugural Westpac Women of Influence Award for Diversity.

Acknowledgements

Storytelling is a uniquely powerful act. To share your story is to make yourself vulnerable, to be exposed. Despite the risks, a writer perseveres in the hope that their story helps someone else: helps them to be brave, to understand, to feel loved and less alone.

Each of the contributors in this beautiful collection has done just that, and I thank them most sincerely. It was a privilege to assist in crafting, editing and publishing their letters. Many refused payment, choosing instead to donate their writing fee to *CARE Australia* – a second act of generosity.

Thank you to the brilliant Lucy Ormonde, without whom the idea for this book would never have been born. The two of us really should go on long walks more often. The streets of Fitzroy North are an underrated location, in which genius can strike at any moment.

I apologise to my editor Cate Blake for taking so long to show her any evidence whatsoever that I was actually working on this manuscript. I am exceedingly grateful for her calm, patience and kindness.

Chloe Davies, bringer of banners, organiser of magnificent events and best publicist in the business deserves all the applause. As do Lou Ryan at Penguin Random House and Christine Gordon at Readings, two people whose support for the next generation of women writers is unmatched.

Sari Braithwaite continues to keep me company while I write in cafes, and the fine folk at Ampersand in Thornbury are yet to complain about their skyrocketing wi-fi bills. Thanks to my mama friends who gave input on cover design, and the incomparable Van Badham, who introduced me to the authors of some of my favourite letters.

My darling Tania Petsinis has always believed in this book and, by the time it goes to print, will be finding it rather useful! Thank you also to the team at Profile Talent and particularly Sarah Dewing, who did the painstaking work of wrangling the biographies and contracts of the contributors.

Clare Bowditch's extraordinarily long SMS lifted me out of the deep, dark hole I'd dug myself during those early weeks of motherhood. What I didn't know then was that she'd be rescuing me from my own thoughts again, two and a half years later, when I was diagnosed with a brain tumour. Clare, your friendship fills me up to the brim. I love you.

Thank you to my family, especially my mother, Helen, to whom this book is dedicated. Mum, please forgive me for everything I ever said or did as a child – I didn't know how hard it was. You did a magnificent job. Mim and I really did win the parent lottery.

And finally, thank you to my son, Rafi. Mate, we had an awfully rocky start to what has since become the best ride of my life. Who knew that fear and panic would give way to such enormous, unbridled, boisterous fun? Thanks for choosing me to be your mum. It is the honour of a lifetime.